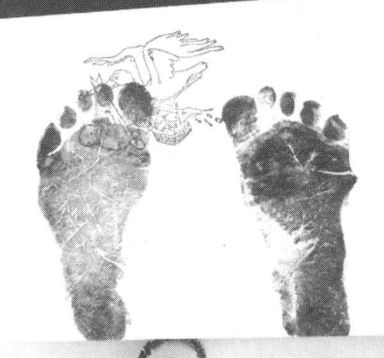

A View from the Parents' Corner
Crayon Marks on a Gutsy Heart

Laura S. Hull

© 2004 Laura S. Hull
Printed by Sheridan Books, Inc.
613 East Industrial Drive, Chelsea, MI 48118
www.sheridanbooks.com

All rights reserved

No part of this book may be reproduced in any form without written permission from the author.

Printed in the United States of America

ISBN 0-9770901-0-8

Table of Contents

Part I: Neon Colors — 1

1. The Udder Truths Of Breast Feeding — 3
2. Pets: The Ark Parked Outside Our House — 11
3. The Toot/Burp Box: The Quest For Good Manners — 19
4. There's A Chuck E. Cheese's In Hell, I Just Know It! — 25
5. The Great Truths Of Parenting — 29

Part II: Primary Colors — 45

6. My Mommy Was Famous! — 47
7. Sex, Lies, And Not A Videotape In Sight! — 55
8. The Alphabetical List Of Dirty Words — 61
9. The Truth About Santa — 67
10. Home For The Holidays — 75
11. Life Is A Beach! — 81
12. The Miracle — 93
13. I Can Show You The World – Traveling With Kids — 101
14. Parenthood: The Great Balancing Act — 127
15. The Buck Stops Here: Raising Kids With Good Character — 135
16. Television/Movie No-No's — 145
17. Toys, Toys, Everywhere! — 153

Part III: Pastel Colors — 159

18. The Story Of Us — 161
19. Fighting Infertility: The Birth Of Chad — 165
20. The Woes Of The First Born — 175
21. The Second Time Around: Joey — 181
22. Battling Lupus: The Birth Of Laurie — 189
23. Our Little Venetian Baby: Zach — 201
24. And Baby Makes Seven: The Birth Of Lanie — 211
25. The Lion, The Monkey, Two Princesses, And A Doodle-Doo — 225

Conclusion — 239

Preface

Several books deal with strong-willed children. This book, however, journals "family" through the eyes of a strong-willed mom.

A View from the Parents' Corner is actually a sequence of three separate views. This 34-year-old mother of five bares her bold, wise, and tender heart.

Like her children's crayon drawings, Laura's reflections are hued in neon, primary, and pastel colors.

The first view, a humorous perspective, reveals a heart colored by shockingly bold neon crayons. You'll definitely laugh, probably gasp, and possibly say, "I can't believe she said that!" The brief neon unit lightly and brightly deals with those stark realities of life your mother never prepared you to face.

The longest unit reveals a wise heart, proudly displayed in primary colors. This enlightening and inspiring collection of lessons learned and lessons taught illustrates purposeful and courageous parenting at its best.

The third section of the book looks at motherhood from a pastel perspective. While many books tell parents what to do, this collection of sweet memories actually shows moms how to feel.

While you may not always agree with the author's opinions, you'll admire her intensity of conviction and the effective way she uses laughter, wisdom, and love to model gutsy parenting.

Peggy Adkins,
Author of the "Exercising Character" series,
and the "What's a Parent to do?" series
for CHARACTER COUNTS!, a project of the Josephson Institute of Ethics

This book is lovingly dedicated to my five precious children: Chad, Joey, Laurie, Zach, and Lanie... "You star in the story of my life." Each of you make my view from the Parents' Corner a beautiful sight to behold. From the moment each of you were born, you put your own special mark on my heart and added beautiful colors to my life. Being your mother is the greatest honor that could have ever been bestowed on me. I'll love you always.

And to my husband, David, my wonderful partner in our parenting corner. Thank you for all your love and support in this project and in every other aspect of our lives. You are my best friend and the love of my life. "I'll be loving you, always... not for just an hour, not for just a day, not for just a year, but always."

To my parents: I learned so much throughout the years from your experiences in the Parents' Corner. Your influence on my life is immeasurable. I wish to express in a very public way my gratitude for the positive impact and effort you make on our family's behalf. My children benefit immensely from their loving relationship with you. It's obvious in the way they feel about you. Thank you for loving my children that way. I love you both very much.

To my sister, Suzanne: Watching you in your new role as a mother has been a delight. You are such a good mother to Blake and he's a lucky little boy to have you. Hold on to every wild and wonderful moment with him, as it goes by way too fast; I know that you will. I enjoy our relationship as both sisters and friends. I love you.

To my sister, Mary Katherine: I had a preview of the Parents' Corner by having the privilege of watching you grow up and having a hand in raising you. You were a beautiful child who grew up to be a beautiful young woman, both inside and out. I love you.

To Christi: You are the big sister I never had. I have always felt that way, and always will. And Robert, you are the brother I never had. Both of you will always have a special place in my heart. "Roll Tide", "Sweet Home Alabama" and I love you.

To Lauren: I am always amazed at your strength and your strong sense of family. You will always be important to me. I love you.

To Kim, Mary Ellen, Sonia, Wendy, and Christina: In a world where people come and go out of each other's lives, we are lucky to find one or two people who are "life friends". I was lucky to be blessed with you. You guys are the "inner circle" for me. Thank you for ALWAYS being there for me. I will always be there for you.

To Pam, thank you for taking a professional relationship into a friendship. I will always be grateful for the role you've had in my life. Please read the chapter about Laurie, and know that I will always be your friend.

To Dana and Debbie, new friendships can be such a blessing...Dana, only another southern gal could understand and encourage my use of the phrases "cool beans", "shindig" and "hollering". You are so cool. Thanks for thinking I'm so cool too! Debbie, my Starbuck's buddy...thank you for being willing to pencil yourself in on my calender and occasionally pulling me away from the things that "have to get done". I think you are great.

To Peggy, thank you for believing in me and my work. Thank you, thank you, thank you!

And to those individuals who helped me see the value of "just putting it out there" and of "writing it all out", I thank you. Your encouragement helped make this labor of love possible.

Introduction To A View From The Parents' Corner

As a thirty something mother of five children, ranging in age from a pre-teen son to an infant daughter, I find myself sitting in the Parents' Corner, absorbing the lessons that life with children inevitably teaches. In college, I remember hearing about birth order, well-defined roles within the family and how they play out within the home. Of course, being an all-knowing, infinitely wise college student, taking an obligatory class in behavior modification, I wrongly perceived our brief study in this area to be a bunch of psycho-babble, bull-la-la, concocted by well-meaning therapists to the tune of $150.00 per hour. It wasn't until a dozen years and five kids later that I learned how little I knew then. As a student in the classroom of my own home, I am confident that I will continue learning for years to come.

Roles within the home are well-defined, and at times absolutely predictable, as girlfriends and I concluded in a recent self-preservation strategy called "girls only night". The sub-sandwiches and fistfuls of chocolate, inspired a lot of girl talk. We unanimously decided to skip the $150.00 therapist fee and revitalized ourselves in a more direct way. The resulting day at a spa, with a young masseur named Jean Claude and cucumber packs on our sleep-deprived, swollen eyes was a weary mom revival. It's amazing how a day at the spa, complete with a mud bath and muscular manipulation can bring such clarity and inner peace! Among the pearls of wisdom we noted that day is that moms are notoriously known as "the spoiler". Moms have a bad reputation for spoiling all the fun.

An example "spoiler" incident involved our oldest son at the tender age of two. Being a young, wide-eyed, first time mother, I eagerly read every book and article I could get my hands on, teaching "how to promote creativity in your child". I must have missed the chapter that dealt with "chocolate pudding fingerprints on your freshly painted white walls!" Needless to say, upon discovering Chad's "artwork", I quickly issued a "cease and desist" order. My son's response was one that was both surprising and profound. He turned to his daddy, and asked in complete seriousness, "Why does Mommy have to quit the fun?" Even at the age of two, he had discovered that I was the one who stood between him and his way, and that he could appeal my decision to the "Higher Court of Daddy". Fortunately, Daddy knows who really sits on the high bench in the court of our home and defers the parenting decisions to me most of the time. However, our children's perception of the roles in our home remain mostly unchanged, even today.

I have a long history of "quitting the fun". Being the primary one in charge of teaching responsibility to our children is often a thankless job and has earned me the reputation of being "one tough Mama". It's not that David doesn't enforce our rules, but I'm the one at home with the kids. Because I spend more hours with the children, I am the one who ends up being the "enforcer" most of the time. I don't believe in a "you just wait until your daddy gets home" form of parenting. Daddy does back up my efforts, but most of the "dirty work" is done by the time he gets home from work. At that point, both he and the kids are ready for some playtime. It's no wonder the kids choose to ride the roller coasters at the theme parks with their Daddy. After all, he's the "fun one." However, the flip side to this great truth is that when the chips are down, the kids want their Mommy. In the hierarchy of the home, Mommy rules most of the time. When feelings are hurt, when the children are sick or injured, when the boogie man visits their dreams, they ask for Mommy.

I have a box of "special things" that is full of sweet little "I love you" notes from my children and beautiful pictures drawn just for me. These precious offerings of love from the heart are among my most treasured material possessions. They may not always see me as the fun one, but I know how much they love me. When they come home with a good grade on a test, or have a special art project they want to show off, they proudly display it for me. It's not that they don't want to show it to Daddy, but they want to show it to me first. This makes me smile.

Yes, the roles within the family are often well defined. Daddy is the fun one. He can fix anything. He can squoosh the bug. He's the tough, yet tender, leader in the family. Mama is the one who often "quits the fun" but is also the bestower of comfort, self-confidence and the leader of the cheerleading section in the child's life. Of course, there are no absolutes to these rules or these roles. The roles of each parent can sometimes cross over those seemingly well-defined lines. But more often than not, these are great truths of parenting, and ones which I often ponder while sitting in the Parents' Corner. Wait! What am I saying? You don't sit in the Parents' Corner! It's where you aggressively engage in the battle of your life, using every resource available (within and without) to assure your child's well-being and development.

Parenthood is a wild and wonderful ride. Each day begins

with eager enthusiasm for what is to come, and each day ends with a profound and wonderful exhaustion in knowing that your day was spent doing something so worthwhile.

Your view from the Parents' Corner will be unique. No two parenting experiences will be exactly the same. These are our stories. This collection will, hopefully, give you a peek into our Parents' Corner, and convey what we feel are the marvelous joys of raising a large family. This is a montage of experiences in my life as the mother of Chad (age 10), Joey (age 8), Laurie (age 5), Zach (age 2 ½) and Lanie (nine months). Each section is independent in purpose. Some of these chapters will illustrate the lessons I've learned about parenting and about life in general. Some chapters will deal with issues every parent faces. And finally, some are just recollections of sweet moments in the lives of my children. I hope you enjoy reading about them, at least half as much as I have enjoyed living them.

Neon Colors

1. The Udder Truths Of Breast Feeding

Oh, for truth in advertising! I'm always amused when seeing articles in pregnancy and parenting magazines on the subject of breastfeeding. They always show a picture of a woman cradling an infant, (a calm infant) to her breast, with a relaxed, unfrazzled look upon her face. Her make-up is on, her hair is perfectly in place, and there's not a milk stain in sight. She always looks well-rested and frankly, she even looks like she probably had a bath that morning. To the first time mother who hasn't slept in weeks (if not months), hasn't bathed in a few days or run a comb through her hair, not to mention the glamorous milk stains on her shirt, the magazine model in this picture depicting the joys of breastfeeding is a deceitful harlot. Okay, she isn't really a woman of ill-repute, but name-calling a magazine illustration is a safe way to vent stress caused by severe sleep deprivation.

A more truthful picture of breastfeeding would be a woman who looks like she has been run over by a truck - a wet dump truck, specifically. At least this would be an accurate picture of the first few weeks after giving birth. Every nursing mother figures out the true meaning of "the boobie trap". It does get much easier as time goes on, but it takes a while for the first time mother to find her groove with breastfeeding. This is an "udder truth" which isn't usually depicted in literature about nursing.

I must admit, as a first time mother just a few weeks shy of my twenty-fourth birthday, I wasn't at all sold on the whole breastfeeding thing. When I became pregnant with our first child, I naturally read as much material as I could about pregnancy and child rearing. I was impressed with all that I read about the benefits of breastfeeding, but I really just couldn't embrace the idea completely. The whole process seemed way too functional and the idea of producing milk made me feel like... well, like a cow! Of course, that just sounds silly now, but in my young mind it just didn't sound sexy. I had just barely made the leap into womanhood and now I was diving head first into motherhood.

The turning point in my perspective on breastfeeding came when I was in my sixth month of pregnancy. An ultrasound confirmed that our son had hydronephrosis in one of his kidneys, which in layman's terms means that one of his kidneys drained too slowly and could make him prone to kidney infections. A significant number of children with this condition eventually outgrow it, and fortunately for us, this was the case with our son. He had outgrown this by his first birthday. However, anytime parents get the news that all is not perfect with their child, it sends fear straight to the heart. David and I consulted a pediatric urologist while I was still pregnant and he advised me to breastfeed, since processing breastmilk is so much easier on the kidneys than baby formula. That settled the issue right then and there... just call me Bessie. I was going to be a milk maiden, and it didn't matter how farm girlish it looked!

Midway through my sixth month of pregnancy, I started leaking colostrum. By the eighth month, I was soaking my shirts at night. I thought this was a little strange, but the nurse at my OB's office assured me that it was perfectly normal and probably indicative of a good milk supply. At 37 1/2 weeks, our beautiful son was born after a whopping thirty minute labor (a little quick for a first time mother!). After getting his APGARs and cleaning him up, the nurse brought over our new little bundle of joy and asked if I wanted to nurse him. I must say, I was still a little shell-shocked from the whole delivery thing and it didn't even cross my mind to nurse him.

"Do you really think he wants to eat?" I asked naively. She just smiled and told me she would help me get him to latch on. Immediately, my sweet baby latched on and sucked ferociously, much like I imagine a little piranha might do. I let out a little shriek of pain, removed him from my breast and searched his mouth for teeth! Upon finding none, I watched him root around for a moment, then let out a soft little cry, which was immediately quieted when he latched back on. He knew exactly what to do, which was a good thing, because I certainly did not. I was absolutely amazed at the way nature provides the instincts for survival, even in these most delicate beings. It touched my heart. "This is a good thing" I thought, and I felt so very bonded with him by being able to meet his needs in this way.

All was going well until we hit the 48 hour mark after delivery. Suddenly a dam broke open (figuratively speaking, of course). I was in the milk-producing business, big time. I generally don't give out a lot of personal information about myself, but for sake of perspective I will tell you that before I got pregnant, I was a 34C. With my milk coming in, I measured in at a whopping 38DD, and the change came literally overnight! I woke up on that third morning ready to compete with the big girls and I didn't even have to pay a plastic surgeon to do it! The lactation consultant at the hospital came to visit me and even she was impressed. "Wow! You've got a lot of milk. You will have no problems breastfeeding."

"Is it normal to leak this much?" I asked. She assured me that in the next few days, supply would meet demand and I would not have as big an issue with it at that point. In the meantime, my son was happily lapping up the wealth and was visibly gaining weight even in those first few days.

The following weeks, I will admit, are pretty much a big blur. The sleep deprivation was profound and I just wasn't prepared for it. As much as I loved being a mom, the fatigue was overwhelming and the days ran together. One concrete memory I do have of those early days was staying wet. When I slept, I soaked the bed. When I fed him on one side, I soaked my clothes from the other side, even though I was wearing pads. I lived on the phone with the lactation consultant, because I knew there was no way this could be normal. If this WAS normal, I didn't know how any nursing mom ever left the house. All I knew was that I was tired to the bone, chronically wet, and had the alluring smell of sour milk on me constantly. Finally, she conceded that I was most likely an overproducer. I was like.. "DUH!" I had enough milk to feed a third world country! She had a few suggestions for me to try to get the situation under control. I am going to do my best to illustrate these solutions, because if you can get a mental picture of these things in your mind, you will laugh out loud!

The first thing she had me do was to try collecting the leaking milk from the side I was not feeding my son from. Picture this if you will... I am sitting on the couch, shirt off, nursing my son on one side. I attach a Playtex plastic nursing bag off of the breast on other side. As my son is eating, I am dripping three to four ounces of milk into a plastic bag. Folks, this was not attractive. I have wondered what David must have thought as he watched his formerly fun-loving wife, dripping milk into a plastic bag, and falling asleep while doing it. I am sure that he didn't recognize the body there, because I certainly didn't. I froze the milk I collected that way, in case it became necessary to use it at a later point. By the time I quit collecting it at six months, I had stored over 300 ounces.

The suggestion that finally got my milk supply under control was bizarre. The lactation consultant suggested that I put damp, raw cabbage in my bra for 24 hours. Apparently, this helps dry up milk, though I never really understood why. Oh my, how quickly life can change. Forget sexy lingerie, I had huge, wet nursing bras stuffed with damp cabbage leaves. It was enough to kill the romance in any marriage. Actually, David was very sweet about the whole thing, and kept assuring me that things would be "normal" again and that he still thought I was hot. But I did not feel hot. I felt fat, tired, and WET! Poor guy, deep down he must have been worried on some level, because I certainly was. I still had twenty pounds to lose, I smelled like spoiled milk and rotten cabbage and I looked like a wreck! But the cabbage worked, and slowly life started to return to normal.

For the most part, nursing continued without a hitch until around the time we introduced solid food. Another udder truth of nursing that most nursing mothers will verify is that the baby often plays favorites with one breast, particularly once breastfeeding is scaled back. All of my children favored my left side. Why? I do not know, but it was true five times. By the time solid foods were the staple in their diets and nursing reduced to just a few times per day, all of my children refused to nurse except on the favorite side. This, of course, leads to a very lopsided chest. I found myself stuffing the right side of my nursing bra with one of my husband's socks and carrying its mate around in my pants pocket, so as to not separate the pair. This worked pretty well and the only time I ever had an embarrassing moment with it was once when the matching sock fell out of my pocket at my friend's house and she asked me why I was carrying one sock around in my pocket. In the grand scheme of things, this was a pretty minor embarrassment, but it was worth a good chuckle at the time.

I nursed my son until he was fifteen months old and I was pregnant with our second child. Upon weaning, I asked David if he was going to miss "the girls upstairs". His answer shocked me. He said "You know, honey, those things are just a little TOO big!" I was floored. I didn't know the bust could be too big from the male perspective. Live and learn!

Fortunately, I did not have problems with overproduction with our other children and nursed all five of them through the first year and beyond. It was very rewarding and our children have experienced good health across the board. I have not tried to be overly discreet about nursing in front of my older children. I want my older sons in particular to know that the female body was made to feed an infant and that is the primary purpose of breasts, though they will hear differently once they enter the teenage years. I don't want the sight of a woman's chest to be titillating for them. (and yes, that pun was intended.)

For the most part, our children have not said much about watching me breastfeed. My second son, Joey, did ask me once why girls have bottles on their chest, while boys have plates. That took a lot of thought, in my opinion. I can only recall two other funny incidents, both involving our daughter Laurie, who is our third child. She was around the age of 2 1/2 when our fourth child was born. Upon coming to the hospital to visit her new baby brother, she studied me intensely while she watched me nurse him for the first time. After a few minutes, she asked me what I was doing. I told her that I was feeding the baby milk. She responded by asking if he was "eating from my udders". Oh my, the udder truth can throw you for a loop!!!! Again, I was feeling pretty functional that day.

Another incident occurred with our daughter shortly after the birth of our fifth child, her baby sister. I was sitting on the couch, nursing the baby, while watching TV. I glanced over at Laurie, sitting on the couch opposite of me, and saw her with her baby doll stuffed up her shirt. I asked her what she was doing. She responded "My baby was hungry, too." That was a reality check for me. Little eyes are ALWAYS watching! Never forget that.

A somewhat negative angle on breastfeeding is that your breasts sag terribly after you wean your baby, particularly if you breastfed for a long period of time. As a child, I had noticed older women whose breasts were sagging so badly they needed to be tucked into their pants. I wondered what in the world could make those things fall so far south. Well, I am in my mid-thirties now, and mine would hang down to my ankles if it were not for a good supportive bra. When I turn 40, my birthday gift to myself will be a tummy tuck and a boob lift. I have already started saving. I don't expect it to be cheap.

Breastfeeding probably isn't for everyone, but it has certainly been a positive experience in our family. Despite the fact that you feel more functional than sensual for a period of time, I wouldn't trade those days with my babies for anything. The udder truth is that those breastfeeding days go by very quickly, but the bonding that results from it lasts a lifetime.

2. Pets: The Ark Parked Outside Our House

Here's a pop quiz: What does Noah of Noah's Ark fame have in common with the Hull family? If you answered: "They both lived with a bunch of different animals" then you would be correct! Treat yourself to an animal cracker! Over the years we have had enough pets in our family to fill up an ark of our own. Have you ever thought about poor Noah? Can you imagine what that ark must have smelled like after 40 days? Were nose clips included in that cruise special? Mercy!

Animals can be a lot of work, even ones that are beloved family pets. I suppose it has been an innate desire in the heart of every child that has ever been born to have a pet. I'm not sure why it's true, but I have never in my life met a child who did not like animals and didn't want a pet. I had a few pets of my own when I was growing up and we even had a pet rabbit the first year we were married. But I usually lost the desire to take care of a pet about 5 minutes after they moved in, and that is even true today in our own home.

I'll be up front and honest. While I recognize the value of child-pet relationships, I am not a pet person. No one would ever mistake me for an animal lover. I am a meat-eating, fur and leather wearing advocate for the "pets are not people, too" movement. Please don't send me angry letters and emails telling me I am a heartless fiend. I would never want to see any animal abused, neglected, or mistreated. But I also do not like to see animals treated as equal to humans and I resent that there are folks out there that treat their animals better than their children.

Okay, I am going to hop off of my soap box and get back to the subject of this chapter. My children have all expressed a desire for a pet at one time or another, and we have had quite a few pass through our home over the years.

Our first attempt at a pet was a small box turtle. Our son Joey named him "Tony"... Tony Turtle. Tony was an interesting little guy. He was fairly interesting to watch as he slowly inched along our patio. He actually lived in an old baby port-a-crib that was filled with mulch. Our boys would take him out twice a day to let him eat and get some exercise. His daily diet consisted primarily of romaine lettuce and strawberries (which he liked very much.) On the weekends, he would get a treat of mill worms. For some reason, these little mill worms creeped my boys out and they refused to touch them or handle them at all. One time, three year old Laurie declared her older brothers were "sissies" and boldly lifted these little creatures out of the dirt and fed them to little Tony. Personally, as far as pets go, I liked Tony. But he had this annoying little habit of pooping in your hand when you held him. It got to the point that the kids really didn't want to handle him at all. My kids quickly lost interest in him after the next pet moved in.

Around Easter time, our church was having its annual Easter egg hunt. Off in the corner of the parking lot, a man with a petting zoo was selling baby bunnies. David committed a major penalty of parenting. He sent our sweet little Laurie over to me while I was talking to a friend. Her new baby bunny was in the sack she was carrying. Her face was just beaming with excitement and delight. WHOA! Flag on the play! Mommy just got blindsided and she never saw it coming! Ooh! Daddy was

A View from the Parents' Corner

going straight to the penalty box! There was no way I was going to tell our precious little Laurie that she could not have the bunny she so proudly had brought over to show me. We did not have a dog house in our back yard, but if we did, David would have surely been logging some time in it! Home we went with our new pet named "Peter"... yes, he was "Peter Rabbit". Tony's days in the Hull home were numbered. If I recall correctly, he lasted for about two more weeks. At that point, we returned him to the pet store and asked them to find him a new home.

Peter was an interesting pet. He grew really big and really fat, really fast. My children really liked him initially. But they soon came to realize that a bunny isn't "just a dog with long ears". They wanted him to play fetch and chase them around the yard. Bunny cages stink badly, really badly...and our kids never wanted to take care of that dirty job. Bunnies poop... a lot. Peter was losing his popularity with the kids, but the straw that broke the camel's back for old Peter was when we let him out on our screen porch for a little exercise. He used his razor sharp teeth to chew holes through the pool net covering our pool, which we had custom made for over $1000.00. I told David that Peter had to find a new home immediately or he was going to be the main ingredient in a homemade stew. Fortunately, someone at David's office took him the next day and I didn't need to warm up my slow cooker.

We were without a pet for a few months before the wails and cries broke out among the kids over the fact that "all of our friends have pets, why can't we have a pet too?" Quickly, we were on to pet number three, but what my kids really, really wanted was a dog. My parents had a little three year old weiner dog that they offered to my kids. He was a sweet little dog, but I felt like we needed a dog just about as much as I needed a bullet to the brain. Finally I caved in to the pressure and agreed to transport this dog from my parents house in Atlanta to our home in Saint Petersburg. Looking back on that now, I must have been experiencing temporary insanity. Why I would ever load up my then four kids and a dog on a five hundred mile car trip is beyond me. First, the dog, named Lucky, hated riding in cars... it made him a nervous wreck. He howled at least the first hundred miles of the trip. Second, the dog had problems with gas emissions... big problems. Have you ever heard about lethal gases that are silent, but deadly? Doggy toots would be right up there amongst the best of them. It was a long, long trip to Florida. I hung my head out of the window for most of the trip. Between his foul bowel and my allergy to dog hair, I was half dead by the time we finally got home. Lucky howled and cried for the first several nights and he wouldn't eat for the first three days. He seemed happy when the kids would come out in the yard to play. By the end of the first week, he had adjusted to his new digs. He was a mischievous little pooch, but my biggest complaint was the little tootsie rolls he left all over the porch.

Shortly after we brought Lucky to our home, I found out that I was pregnant with our fifth child. I'll admit, had I known that I was pregnant, I would have never agreed to take the dog home. But given the fact that he was already with us, we tried to make the best of the situation. In the beginning, the kids were eager to feed and walk the dog and spent a lot of time with him. But as the newness began to wear off, they started coming up with excuses for not taking care of him. Eventually, I had to assign feeding times to the boys and the time they spent with

Lucky began to sharply decrease. David and I began to feel we would not be able to manage Lucky once the new baby arrived. We were not ready to throw in the towel at that point, but we were certainly beginning to have our doubts.

The next couple of months went by and the fact that we had a dog to take care of, on top of everything else going on in our lives, just didn't make sense. Eventually, our older boys, Chad and Joey, started shirking their responsibilities and we planned to find Lucky a new home once the baby arrived. However, Lucky became willful and disobedient. Our next door neighbors have a pit bull and Lucky would stand next to our fence and bark fiercely at the dog next door. I pictured in my mind that dog leaping over my fence and making short order of our little weiner dog. Our dog was all bark and no bite. Their dog, I was sure, was all bite.

This little dog was sweet, but not particularly smart and I found myself wanting to smack him on the nose frequently (though I never actually did). When I was five months pregnant, I was driving home from dropping off my three older children at school. As I approached my house, I saw Lucky just standing in the middle of my driveway. He had dug out from under the fence and was waiting in the front yard. I slowly approached the driveway in my car, cut the engine and moved slowly out of my car. I stared straight at my dog and he stared straight back. Slowly, slowly I approached him, and then it happened... BAM! He took off down the street! Our 18 month old, Zach, was still strapped in his carseat (fortunately) and the car was locked. So, off I went after him. Picture in your mind, if you will, a very pregnant and VERY ANGRY mother running down the street, chasing a very fast little weiner dog, that is heading straight for a very busy street. I was screaming at the top of my lungs for him to stop, to "come back here," but he ignored me... he never looked back, he never even broke stride. Fortunately, a group of construction workers, who were working down the street, saw this whole scene and chased Lucky down for me. This was the last straw. I returned home, put Lucky in his crate, and called David. I told him the dog would have to go... immediately. I knew that he would not be safe in our yard. If he dug out once, he would dig out again. And if I happened to not be home, he would likely wander into traffic, or equally as bad, he would dig into the next door neighbor's yard and get eaten alive by their pit bull.

I was not really heartsick to find a new home for Lucky, but I felt really bad for my children that we were getting rid of yet another family pet. I called a local office in town that I knew was really pet friendly and asked them if they knew anyone who wanted our dog. Within an hour, I received a call back saying they had found Lucky a home and it was with a family that already had another weiner dog. I knew this would be a much better situation for Lucky and certainly a better situation for us. But I knew this was not going to be an easy thing for the kids to understand, and I was dreading the conversation.

When the kids came home from school that day, I gave them the bad news. For the most part, Chad and Laurie took it pretty well. Joey, however, did not. "But you can't get rid of Lucky, Mommy!" he said. "He's a part of our family. We can't just get rid of a part of our family." He was in tears and my heart was breaking for him. I knew that in his mind, if we could so easily get rid of Lucky, what was to stop us from getting rid of one of them? I called a therapist and asked her what would be the best way to handle this. I was hoping that she might have some profound words or an approach that would make this easier. But for the most part, she just re-affirmed what I already knew... that I needed to re-assure him that Lucky was going to a home where he would be happy and that Joey's place (and the place of his siblings) would always be with us, and that it was okay to be sad. For the most part, Joey refused to be consoled and he grieved more than all the siblings combined. We promised him that we would get them a new pet, one better suited for our home. I know, as you read this you are probably asking yourself, "Don't those people know when to quit? I mean, how many times have they been beaten with a stupid stick?"

Next, we decided to invest in an aquarium; a very large aquarium. This was around the time that "Finding Nemo" was still so popular at the movies, and we decided to buy the fish from the movie. These were quite expensive, delicate little fish, and we had no experience in the upkeep of a tank. The short version of this story is that we managed to kill them all within the first month of our new experiment. This did not go over well with the kids, especially Joey. Back to the pet store we went to look for new fish.

This time I spotted something very unique... a stingray. I thought this was pretty cool. I mean, how many kids have a pet stingray? The people at the pet store told me that stingrays are pretty hardy, so we took him home. "Butch" was big and interesting, but appeared very lazy. He mostly wanted to bury himself in the sand, and I became bored with him in a few days. At $75.00, I figured we could find a more interesting fish. I announced that we would take him back and exchange him for something else. That's when it all broke loose. Joey declared "YOU GET RID OF ALL MY PETS!" and burst into tears. "Okay, okay.." I said. "We will just keep him." I figured that a $75.00 stingray was cheaper than paying for the future therapy he would need if I took away just one more pet. Butch ended up being a pretty cool pet. When he did swim around, he was quite interesting. One day, when I went to school to have lunch with Chad, one of the boys in his class asked me "Does Chad really have a pet stingray?" "Yes, he does." I said. Immediately, this kid yelled down the table "Chad REALLY DOES have a pet stingray!" There was a collective "Oooh!" that spread over the table. Chad was proud of his pet, and I felt good for him that his friends saw his pet (and him) as "cool". Butch stayed in our home until he died of old age, and we have moved on to a pet porcupine puffer fish named "Porky" and a chainlink eel named "Willie". They are cute to watch, and really not much trouble as far as pets go. I think we may have found our "pet niche" with this aquarium and all the kids seem happy with our "newest additions" to the family.

In future editions of this book, I am sure that this section will need to be updated, but for now, all is well on the ark parked in front of the Hull house...and there's not a rain drop in sight!

3. The Toot/Burp Box: The Quest For Good Manners

I find that one of the most daunting tasks facing parents today is trying to raise polite, well-mannered children. I find it to be especially difficult to raise polite boys. I recall a poem I heard as a child that went something like this... "What are little boys made of? What are little boys made of? Snakes and snails and puppy dog tails. That's what little boys are made of." Not a very flattering picture, huh? Now how do you suppose little boys got such a bad rap? Mud pies, potty noises, and bug catching is probably where it started, but that is certainly not where it ends.

I remember having a rush of thoughts lying on the ultrasound table, when they told me that our first child would be a boy. The first things that came to mind were soccer games, years at the ball field, jock straps...and I kid you not...I pictured a little blond-haired boy with his hand cupped under his arm making potty noises. I grew up in a family of all girls and these were the only images of little boys I had. "I will raise a wonderfully mannered little guy." I thought to myself. And the picture in my mind shifted away from the little guy making arm noises, to a spit-shined, rosy-cheeked little fella with a "Young Republican" haircut.

I'll tell you straight up. There is nothing that is more of a turn off for me than seeing a rude child with no manners. Parents have gotten away from teaching good manners in the home and I think this is a real disservice to our children. Children (and adults, for that matter) are showing respect when using good manners; respect not only for the feelings of others, but also showing respect for themselves. It is holding themselves to a higher standard of behavior than a lot of people choose to display. Good manners are an attractive quality for any child, but I think it is especially so with boys, because they tend to be more aggressive by nature. When a child has good manners, people notice. When a child has terrible manners, people notice even more. This is why we work so hard in our family to drive home the importance of good manners. I have to brag on my kids. They have really nice manners... they say "please and thank you" without having to be prompted. They say "excuse me" instead of interrupting a conversation, and they are very respectful of the authority of adults and of the feelings of their friends. I frequently hear from the adults who interact with my children that they are some of the most polite, well mannered children they have seen. This always makes me so proud.

For the most part, I would say that their manners are almost perfect... with only one exception. Candor demands that I reveal our dark family secret for the first time today. My kids think that digestive noises are a real hoot! I am hiding my face in shame as I type. The truth is ugly (and at times even smelly) and we've implemented a few tricks that have helped us keep it under control. One of the most effective tools we have is our "toot/burp" box. Haven't seen one of these little gems at Wal-Mart? Well, I'm not surprised. This is a Hull family original (or at least as far as I know it is original). I am only sharing this in hope that our strategies in this area might work for you.

For some reason, children think that any odd noise that comes out of a body opening is way too funny... and the louder, the better. This is especially true for my boys. Between our boys, their friends, and their sister (when she would participate), my house was turning into a "gas-passing Grand Central Station". If they could not muster "the real deal" then they would supplement the activities with a little under arm action or a quick blow into the hands. Immediately, there is laughing and congratulations for the biggest sounding, longest lasting or worst smelling. If my daughter is the least bit competitive, it brings her up a notch in her brothers eyes and she's allowed to hang out with them for a little while longer.

My daughter's participation in these little shenanigans is particularly disturbing. Laurie is as dainty and feminine as any little girl I have ever seen. But she thinks burps and toots are really funny as well. One time she let one rip (on purpose) much to the delight of her brothers. I asked her "Why did you do that?" She declared, "Tooting is my power!" like it was some kind of superhero thing, like x-ray vision or flying with a cape. I asked her, "What do you mean when you say it is your power?" "When I toot, everyone falls down!" she replied. "Good grief!" I thought to myself. "So this is what happens when you have two older brothers teaching you "the ropes." I pointed out to her that her favorite princesses do not behave this way. I asked her "Do you think Cinderella toots in front of the prince?" Heaven's no! "Does Barbie burp in front of Ken when they are having a pool party?" Put in terms she can relate to, she can see the error of her ways. Of course, her brothers are always quick to point out that everyone does it... princesses, included.

My boys think it's so funny when the baby lets loose. Those little babies can deal out some that are quite explosive! In some ways, this has been a bonding mechanism; sort of a club initiation. After all, if she is going to be a member of our tribe she had better know how to turn it loose! It's a losing battle for a mother like me... five little toots up against one fumigator. Now I can't imagine what could be the least bit funny or appealing about these antics, particularly in front of friends, (eg: pull my finger) but every kid I have ever known has participated. (My own mother says I am not the exception to the rule, but I have no memory of it, thank goodness. I DO, however, remember my sister Suzanne was an unusually gifted belcher who could burp to the tune of the "Dallas" tv show's theme music on cue. I do remember thinking this was both cool and weird.)

With five children, I could see the potential of this getting way out of hand in our home. One day the kids came home from school and were introduced to a new concept... the toot/burp box. This is how it works: If one of the kids (or their daddy!) burps without saying excuse me, lets one rip on purpose or without saying excuse me or obnoxiously keeps imitating noises to the point of causing the other kids to laugh so hard that they actually do toot, then they have to pay the box a quarter... a really heinous offense might cost them a dollar. You have to understand, we have a monetary reward/demerit system in our home. The kids earn money by making good grades and helping me around the house. I buy toys at Christmas and on birthdays. If they want a new toy outside of these times during the year, they often must buy it with their own money. One form of discipline in our home does involve money. This is where the box comes in. I do not think that bad manners necessarily require disciplining our children with groundings, time-outs, or spankings. I have found the "payment to the box" to be very effective. It pains my kids to have to give up their hard-earned money.

A View from the Parents' Corner

Digestive noises, whether real or imitation, aren't quite as funny when they cost a quarter a piece.

Actually, we found the toot/burp box to be so effective that we decided to expand on the idea. If I had a nickel for every time my kids have said the word "poop", I'd be writing this book from the Italian Riviera instead of St. Petersburg, Florida. And they like to say it for no other reason than just to say it. For some reason they think it is an extremely funny word. I decided about a year ago, after an hour long car trip with my kids, in which they sang and laughed about this word the whole way home, that going forward, the use of it would require payment into the box. They can only use this word if it is necessary in relaying information. For example, acceptable uses of the word... "Mom, I need to go to the bathroom, I really need to..." or "Mom, I think the baby went.... in her diaper." Unacceptable uses of the word would include singing "poop" over and over to the tune of the Star Wars Theme music. And yes, that really did happened. I just felt like my 10 and 8 year old sons are too old to take such delight in using a potty word... you know what I mean? Who knows, maybe they still talk about it when I am not in ear shot. Maybe they talk about it while firing off a few rounds of bean-backed ammunition. If they do, at least they are savvy enough not to do it when I am around. I do know for sure, however, that the monies I collect in our "box" will surely go a long way toward financing the college education of my well-mannered children who can't resist a good laugh!

A View from the Parents' Corner

4. There's A Chuck E. Cheese's In Hell, I Just Know It!

Oh, the things we will do for our children! We would walk barefoot on hot coal, journey to the ends of the earth, endure the worst that the world can throw at us, if only it will make our children's lives happier. But alas! Even the most enduring, seasoned parent will have to stare straight in to the pit of hell, withstand mental torture and physical challenges and be strong enough to survive to tell the story. Of course, I am referring to obligatory trips to Chuck E. Cheese's. Please, Mr. Cheese, don't take this personally, but an afternoon in your establishment is about as pleasurable to an adult as a protoscope exam. I haven't seen a Biblical reference to it, but if hell is what you dread most in this life, then there is probably a Chuck E. Cheese's down south.

Okay, I guess in all fairness, I should say that it really isn't just Chuck E. Cheese's, it's all of those arcade/pizza type places. These "centers of fun" are places of complete sensory overload. From the time you enter the door, you are bombarded with flashing lights coming from obnoxiously loud video/arcade machines. There are at least 50 kids to every one adult, and every one of them is running... and screaming. I have been to college football games that aren't as loud as these places on a Friday night. I have never met a kid who didn't love these places, and I've never met a parent who does.

In having five children, we have been invited to MANY birthday parties. It happens at least a handful of times per year that someone invites my kids to one at Chuck E. Cheese's. I cringe when I read the invitation. A two hour birthday party at Chuck E. Cheese's is like an afternoon in purgatory for me. "Can't we just skip this one, guys?" I'll ask. "We will take a present over to his/her house," I offer. "Wouldn't you rather do something else?" I plead. The answer is always "No!" I'll usually try one last time... "I'll take you for ice cream... I'll buy you a new toy... I'll buy you your own pony!" Nothing works. They would rather go to Chuck E. Cheese's than to breathe! But being the enduring, seasoned parent that I am, I have learned to just suck it up and keep repeating in my mind "It's only two hours, I can stand anything that makes my kids happy for just two hours! I think I can, I think I can, I think I can..."

At the establishment, we get our hands stamped with matching numbers, then my kids trot off to join the rest of the stampede inside the game room. There are kids everywhere... zipping, running, skipping, hollering. No one seems capable of speaking in an indoor voice. To add insult to injury, there is always blaring music playing over the loud speakers, perhaps in an attempt to drown out the video games and the screeching kids. There always seems to be a great race to each and every game in the establishment. Looking around at the parents in the herd is always interesting. None of the parents are ever smiling... ever. We all resemble a herd of stupid cattle, wandering around aimlessly, while our kids are "defending the universe" on one game or another. My kids will run up to me long enough to beg for more tokens, then ask me to scram if their friends want them to come play a two player game.

It is very easy to blow through a small fortune in tokens, in a really short time. Sometimes one of my kids will ask me to play skee-ball. This is actually kind of fun. It's very easy to keep feeding tokens into the skee-ball machine. If you have even a morsel of success, you just can't resist the urge to keep collecting those tickets, which brings me to another gripe point—have you ever paid much attention to the prizes they offer the kids in return for the tickets "won"? Laurie turned in over 100 tickets one time, which represented at least $10.00 in tokens. They gave her a Kellogg's rice crispy treat! I am dead serious. My daughter won a $10.00 rice crispy treat. Still she was happy with her "prize." I felt like I had just taken a swift kick in the pants (not to mention the wallet).

I have to hand it to Mr. Cheese. He is no dummy. To open a business that is marketed to kids (note-kids have no money of their own), fill it up with money-eating, loud machines, charge fifteen bucks for a piece of cardboard covered with tomato sauce and a token offering of cheese (passed off as "pizza"), and FINALLY to give the child a $10.00 rice crispy treat as a "prize" is quite a business coup. Someone within the Cheese organization is a marketing genius. Let me ask you, is it just a coincidence that Chuck E. Cheese is a rodent? Hmmm...it does make you wonder, doesn't it?

Well, anyway, I guess the final insult in patronizing one of these establishments is walking away with some type of illness. Why do people think it is okay to bring a sick child with fever, a green nose, or an upset stomach to a place full of kids? I know how frustrating it is to be couped up in the house with a sick child, and how tempting it is just to get out for a few minutes and have some fun. But I cannot tell you how many times we have gone to Chuck E. Cheese's, and other places like it, only to have awakened the next morning with a fresh cold or a stomach virus. Of course, I cannot prove that this is where they have picked up illnesses, but the likelihood is very high. All you have to do is look around... kids sneezing and coughing all over the games and tables. And this is not Chuck E. Cheese's fault. The fault lies squarely with the thoughtless and inconsiderate parents of these sick kids. I finally started carrying Lysol wipes with me and began to wipe down the games before I let my children play. I also carry a bottle of Purell around with me and squirt my children's hands frequently. I know this sounds obsessive, but it really does seem to help. My kids have not gotten sick after one of these outings in a long time.

I know we have many more visits to log in with Mr. Cheese; with five children, it is inevitable. I view it the same way I view having expensive, painful dental work... it isn't fun, it's a major pain (literally and figuratively), the time goes by slowly, and you are sure you are paying the price for past sins, but you do it because you must. When you have kids, you have to visit Chuck E. Cheese's. I think it is rule 522A in the great book of parenting rules. I am sure there are worse, more painful things in life. Though I can't recall them right now, I am sure they do exist!

I have now spent an entire chapter on a tangent. But the grand point of this rambling is... as parents we do things for our kids just to see the joy in THEIR faces. Even if that means an afternoon at Chuck E. Cheese's!

A View from the Parents' Corner

5. The Great Truths Of Parenting

There are certain "GREAT TRUTHS" of parenting. There are things that are true no matter where or when the parenting experience takes place. In the secret society of parenting woes, these are great truths to which any parent can relate.

Rule one: Anything that can be served on a plate, can and will be dipped in ketchup. (please note: there are no exceptions to this rule.)

Mealtime is a real test of will on our children's part, and a real test of patience on mine. Cooking for a family of seven is no easy chore, especially when the palate of each child is so different. There are a few staples that all the kids can accept. Everyone will eat macaroni and cheese, pizza, hamburgers, chicken, pb&j and anything made from a potato. Beyond these offerings, meals get tricky. As you would probably agree, these "favorites" are not necessarily the best choices from a nutritional standpoint. Each one of the kids has a few "better" choices that he or she will eat. The problem is, that not all of the kids like these same "better" choices. This leaves virtually every meal with a scowl on someone's face and me wishing I had not put so much effort into the meal's preparation.

A few years ago, David and I starting enforcing the "three bite rule". We don't expect our kids to lick their plates clean at every meal, but anyone can eat three bites of anything, whether they like it or not. This is not a popular rule, and we've actually had children sit at the dinner table for over an hour, waiting to finish his/her three bites. I only re-heat twice. After that, if it's cold, well... you get the point.

Guilt-tripping the kids into eating just doesn't work. The old "starving kids in Africa" line gets the "I don't think they would want your broccoli casserole either" response. And if they really don't like what we are having, they are more than willing to go to bed hungry... and that has happened a few times, too.

I have to admit, sometimes their efforts to "choke down" the dinner are amusing to watch. I require my kids to eat broccoli. In some circles, this would be considered cruel and unusual punishment. But this is so nutritionally important, we don't bend on this one. Chad likes broccoli so it's never an issue for him (onions are his downfall). But Joey and Laurie cannot stand broccoli. Laurie can chew a single bite of broccoli for an hour and nothing can coax her into swallowing. She usually chooses the "no dessert" option rather than eat her broccoli. Now, Joey is a schmoozer who will profess his love for it, but only to score brownie points. He will hold his breath, stuff his mouth to the point of flowerets hanging out and chase it down with a glass of water. More recently, he has taken to dipping it in ketchup. UGH! This brings me to another point. We go through A LOT of ketchup in our house. Our kids will dip anything in ketchup, I kid you not. There is not a food that is safe from their dipping habits.

I have not spoken with any mother of multiple children who has not had big time issues with meals and diets in their homes. I wish I had some great pearls of wisdom or advice to pass on in regards to this subject. Unfortunately, in our home, I have already conceded defeat. I will continue to cook healthy meals, but I have long ago given up the dream of any of my children actually appreciating them.

Rule two: The housework is an unconquerable foe. In the battle of housekeeping, the house always wins. The main culprit is the laundry. I stand at the base of the mountain of laundry and know that I shall never reach the summit! There is no chore I dread more than laundry. I would rather clean the toilet with a toothbrush than fold and put away laundry. Picture if you will, in a family of seven... every day... seven towels, seven washrags, seven pairs of socks, seven pairs of underwear, seven shirts, seven pairs of pants, plus the many outfits the baby soils in a day. There are also sheets, blankets, and any other washable odds and ends that go into the washing machine. Last year, we actually broke down and bought a second set of washers and dryers. I was so excited to have a second set, as this has cut the actual washing and drying time in half. But, of course, the amount of laundry has not decreased. It's only ready to be folded and put away faster. No matter what else I have to do in the course of a day, I always know that there is a pile or two (or ten) of laundry just waiting for me to fold. There have been a few times when I have devoted literally hours to folding and putting away everything in the laundry room. This has given me a very brief feeling of accomplishment. However, it's only a matter of a few hours before a new pile of clothes waiting to be washed begins to accumulate and the whole cancerous process starts over again. My mother accuses me of taking in the neighbor's laundry when she sees the massive piles waiting to be folded. Recently, my youngest sister moved to town to attend college and she began bringing her laundry over as well... need I say more?

Fortunately, our three older children do help me fold and put away laundry, but such a large job rarely gets marked off the "to do" list as a task completed. I always manage to get the clothes washed and dried. We rarely have piles of dirty clothes lying around. We do however frequently have piles — mountains really — of clean clothes lying around. Our older children end up wearing the same three outfits week in and week out because they come pull them out of the dryer and dress themselves in the morning. They have few clothes in their drawers, because everything is waiting in baskets to be folded. There have been times when I would rather just throw the clothes away and buy them again (or perhaps burn a few loads) than to sort through them. Of course, I would never actually do that, but the thought has crossed my mind.

No one would ever accuse me of being an excellent housekeeper. My house is never "dirty", but is frequently cluttered. My kitchen floor does occasionally "crunch" from a stray cheerio or fishy cracker, and you would never walk through my house at night in the darkness because of the danger of stepping on a stray block or some other toy. I used to be much more concerned with the appearance of my house than I am now. I had gotten into the habit of not having my friends over because my house was a wreck. Then, I finally decided that my real friends would not care if my house was a wreck. Anyone who would think worse of me because I am not a great housekeeper probably isn't much of a friend anyway. (and definitely not a mother of five!)

I finally learned to let the housework go, at least some times, in favor of plain ol' fun. I give myself permission to leave a cluttered house behind to go play at the beach

A View from the Parents' Corner

or go to Disney World or wherever our hearts lead us. I know that the housework will always be waiting for me when I get back, but the days of young childhood are rapidly passing by. One day, when I am old, getting ready to leave this world, I don't think my children will surround my bed, hold my hand and say "Gee, Mom, I really wish you had kept a better house when we were young!" I hope they will say something along the lines of... "You remember when Mom got out in the yard and played with us?" or "Remember when she took us to Disney World? Mom spent time with us and she loves us."

It is okay to concede defeat in the battle with housework. Of course, this is not giving us permission to completely dismiss our obligations around the house. Things still have to get done, but it is okay to put them aside for a little while, on occasion, to pursue the more important things in life... family time being the most important.

Rule three: Any promises you make to your children can and will be used against you... frequently! There have been so many examples of this I could reference, I hardly know where to begin. Often, I make deals with the kids at the beginning of an outing, for example: "If everyone cooperates and behaves nicely while we are in the store, we will go for ice cream on the way home." This is a deal I cut frequently with my children. Taking five children, even five well-mannered children like mine, into a busy store for a long period of time is risky business. I always hold my breath that the baby doesn't need a diaper change or that my two year old doesn't have a complete meltdown when we pass by the cookie aisle without picking up a box. By the time I've bought groceries for a week, we have usually been in the store for well over an hour. This is a long time for five kids to mind their P's and Q's in this type of environment, and usually they do great. I must admit, even when the shopping experience is mostly uneventful, I am worn out from it and ready to just head straight home when it is over. A few times I have tried to drive straight home without holding up my end of "the deal." The kids notice every single time. There is a collective outcry from the back of the van: "BUT MOMMY... YOU PROMISED!" So I turn my mammoth-sized van around in the driveway and head back out. Our kids are like elephants... they never forget ANYTHING!

I try hard not to make any promises, of any size, unless I can follow through in a timely manner. My strong-willed determination to put off following through on my promise is never worth the whining I have to endure. Is whining an art form? If so, our kids are masters. If we as parents are to be models of behavior for our children, then we better follow through on our promises, no matter how small they are, if we want our children to learn to promising -keeping. There are times, of course, when following through on a promise must be delayed because unforeseen circumstances make it necessary. When this happens, the reasons should be explained to the children in a way they can understand. Give them another time to expect you to follow through, and then do it.

A footnote about this rule... when children ask you a question along the lines of "Can we do this___?" or "Can we have this?" Answer with a decisive yes or no. "Maybe", "We'll see" and "Let me think about it" is interpreted in little minds as "YES!"

Rule four: Kids disagree with each other just to disagree.

A View from the Parents' Corner

For the most part, my children get along very well, especially given the fact they are so close in age and must share so many things. But there are times, particularly if there has been a lot of "togetherness" in the day, that the bickering begins. I must admit, I have grown rather immune to it. The bickering must be virtually in my face for me to even notice it. I am a big proponent of "You guys work out your own disagreements." If I got into the middle of every disagreement my children had, I'd be refereeing to some degree all day long. As long as no one is in tears (REAL tears) or presents a bloody nose, I generally let them work it out on their own.

Learning to resolve conflict is an important skill for children to possess, and that is why I don't step in unless I absolutely must. There have been times when the noise level has risen to the point that I've sent my children to opposite ends of the house, but that has only happened a few times. Mostly the kids disagree about insignificant things, like what flavor ice cream to buy at the store. (It is always split down the middle... half want vanilla, half want chocolate. Bless the man who invented the box with both — no doubt a wise man, with a lot of kids). Our kids argue about which Disney theme park to visit. (A suggestion along the lines of "Why don't we just stay home today and do some yard work" is usually enough to settle that argument quickly). I think kids just like to argue in general. There really doesn't have to be a "real" reason other than just wanting to yank on a siblings chain, or perhaps exert some control in the tribe. I don't consider this a big problem in our family, but I know this issue exists in every home with multiple children. It just goes with the territory.

Rule Five: No matter how much you buy your child in the way of entertainment, your child's best friend has toys that are "way cooler". (Note: This rule applies even if the friend has the SAME toy, only in a different color!) I really don't even have to elaborate on this rule! The grass is always greener... Do we ever really outgrow this one?

Rule six: Car trips with kids (even across town) are a test of endurance. Whenever we load up our crew for anything longer than a trip to the grocery store, I always hold my breath. It is risky business to confine five children into the tight space of a vehicle — even a mega-vehicle like our conversion van — for extended periods of time.

I still remember the cute little car I had before we had children. I drove a little Saab 900s, a five-speed with a moonroof and a good sound system. Little did I know that driving a five speed would be such an issue once we had children. What a shock it was to find out that it is nearly impossible to shift gears and insert a pacifier in a crying baby's mouth at the same time! We quickly graduated to a family sedan, then to a Suburban when baby three came along. I was really in love with my Suburban until one of my best friends brought over her new conversion van. It had room to stand, seating for seven, and was decked out with a thirteen inch television and dvd player. I'll admit, I was jealous and coveted my friend's van badly. I just knew her car trips were easier than mine.

I am sure that car trips are some form of payback for past wrongs that you THINK you got away with but are suffering for now. "He's touching me!" "He sneezed on me!" "Mommy, he's sitting too close to me!" "Mommy, he's bugging me!" "MOMMY! HE'S LOOKING AT ME!"

A View from the Parents' Corner

Oh no! Anything but that! The whine factor is more of an issue in this setting than in any other in our family. Something about sitting in a car brings out the horns and tails in all of us. There have actually been times when I have thought to myself "I don't see the flames licking my body, but I am pretty sure we are in hell!" Eventually, when our Suburban began developing problems, we purchased a conversion van of our own. I really do like the entertainment package in this unit, and I do carefully monitor what they watch. It helps keep the peace on both short runs across town and on longer trips. Of course, our van is always, always, ALWAYS a mess. There are currently twenty four stickers on my daughter's window courtesy of visits to the pediatrician's office over the last three years (they give two or three at a time. Isn't that nice of them!?) There is always the overpowering smell of old French fries, probably ground into the seats. This is really beyond anything that vacuuming and air freshener can help.

Sometimes, when I am climbing into my big honking van, I wonder what ever happened to my cute little Saab. When we pull into a theme park parking lot, we are often offered handicap parking because of the kind of vehicle it is. I never pictured myself driving this "milk truck" when I was scooting around town in my little sporty car. But I wouldn't have it any other way. The only problem with this seven seater van is if we ever have any more children, we would most likely need to graduate to a bus. The Partridge Family, maybe?

Rule seven: When you have many children, you are helping significantly reduce the medical school debt of your children's pediatrician. I really like my children's pediatrician. She's nice, I think she is smart. She listens to my instincts about our children, which I appreciate. However, as much as I like her, I feel as if I see far too much of her.

Wintertime is hard on a houseful of young children, and I often feel like I live in the doctor's office. The time and money spent in our pediatrician's office is enormous. I have joked with the staff that they need to set aside a suite just for our family, or at least set me up a cot for when I camp out there all winter with our younger children. Fortunately, the older three children are at the age when they really don't get sick that often anymore. But our younger two children seem to always get the cold of the week or the bug of the month. I feel like I wear out a path between my house and the doctor's office until each child reaches the age of three, at which time his immune system seems to mature. We try to contain illnesses as best as we can. I am a little anal about using anti-bacterial spray on household surfaces, and I have bottles of soapless hand sanitizer all over the house and in my car. Any illness that passes through all seven of us can literally take weeks to get out of the house. Last winter, we took our family to get ice cream, and we all sampled each other's flavors. That's a mistake we only had to make once. Unfortunately, unbeknownst to us, my oldest son was carrying strep throat. This spread like wildfire throughout our house, and we were all very sick, at various points, for several weeks. Children really do bring a lot of illnesses into the home, particularly once they are school age. This is just a fact of life when you have children, and the adults in the house tend to also get sick more often because of the higher degree of exposure to contagious illnesses in close quarters.

A View from the Parents' Corner

On our tenth wedding anniversary, David and I had chartered a boat for a sunset cruise to renew our wedding vows. Around lunch time that day, I received a call from Joey's school saying he had suddenly become ill. I picked him up and immediately took him to the doctor. He had a case of hand, mouth, foot disease... a particularly nasty illness, that makes you extremely sick for several days. Feeling he was just too sick to leave with a babysitter, we scrapped our anniversary plans that day. (We ended up rescheduling two months later). This kind of stuff happens when you have kids. Though it was disappointing to have to cancel our plans, it was just par for the course. You have to be flexible and understanding when it comes to things like this. They happen in every home at some point.

I am on a first name basis with the whole staff at my children's pediatrician's office. I figure, if my money is paying off school loans, paying staff salaries and putting the doctor's kids through prep school, they are familiar enough with me to call me by my first name. Okay, that's a little bit of an exaggeration, but not much of one.

Rule eight: Parents, "Thou shalt embarrass your children, frequently". My two older boys are at the age when they think that Mom and Dad are old codgers, "way not cool" and they are embarrassed by us very easily. I have to do nothing more than just open my mouth and sing to embarrass my kids. I'll admit, I can't carry a tune in a bucket. This is very ironic for someone who had the pipes to work in radio, and the ability to play several musical instruments. My kids know that I can't sing, too. Any attempts on my part to sing along with the radio in the car are met with groans of protest... "Stop singing, Mom!" is the outcry from the back seats. One time Laurie said in a very gentle way "Mommy, you know, you really don't sing very good." My sweet-hearted Joey, in an attempt to cushion the blow said, "Yeah, she can't sing, but she can sure cook good!" Leave it to Joey, our little politician in the making, to make lemonade out of lemons. I have used my vocal impairment to my advantage at times, along the lines of "You guys play nice when your company comes over, or I'll sing in front of your friends!" This works every time!

No one would ever mistake me for "hip" and "with it". I still use the phrase "cool beans" which no one has really used since the early 1990's. My own mother had to tell me what "dissing" someone means, and I have only recently become re-acquainted with current music, thanks mostly to my son. As you can probably imagine, my boys cringe at my attempts to seem cool. I must admit, I do have fun razzing the boys in harmless situations. David and I started greeting each other with a loud, obnoxious "Whazzup!" with the appropriate response being "WORD! baby." My boys just roll their eyes into the back of their heads and laugh. Some thrills are just way too easy.

Joey is a very gifted dancer. He is double-jointed like me, but has far more rhythm than I ever dreamed of having. He started taking hip-hop lessons this year and he excels in it. He looks very natural dancing in his classes, and has absolutely no trouble hamming it up for his classmates when he is in the spotlight. Something about dancing at home, however, makes him very uncomfortable and it's amusing to watch. One evening I had David play the song "Bust A Move", an old dance song from at least fifteen years ago. It is a really fun song to dance to, and I tried to coax Joey into dancing with me. No such luck. So, I

A View from the Parents' Corner

decided to do a few little dance moves right there in the kitchen while he and his daddy just stood there. David got a big kick out of the whole thing, but Joey looked like he could have died from embarrassment. "Stop it! Stop dancing right now!" he insisted. Seeing this spark of embarrassment coming from my son, who traditionally is a hambone, was too much of an invitation to pass up. My husband decided to get in on the act. So picture this: two thirtysomething, rhythmically-impaired parents, "busting a move" in grossly exaggerated form, much to the displeasure of their disbelieving children. Okay, I know it was childish, and a cheap thrill at best, but it was harmless fun and we all had a good laugh about it.

Sometimes, my husband and I will "smoochie" in front of the kids, because they think it is so funny and embarrassing. "Quit trying to smoochie our mommy!" the kids will demand from their daddy. "Okay, then I guess we will have to get all of YOUR sugar instead!" and off the chase begins with each child getting a face full of sugar and all the harmless embarrassment they can stand, without wetting their pants with laughter.

A more serious embarrassment breach occurred recently, however, when I committed the cardinal sin of saying "I love you, Sweetie" to my oldest son in front of his friends. This "embarrassment" was not one I committed intentionally. I had gone in to the school early one morning to speak with Chad's teacher for our required quarterly conference. By the time our conference was over, the students were beginning to file into class. As I was leaving, I turned to Chad instinctively, and said "have a good day... I love you, Sweetie!" He just looked at me and said "Okay, bye Mom" in a matter of fact tone of voice.

"Chad!" I said. "Did you hear me? I said I love you". He just grinned and said "I know" and turned away as the late bell was ringing. I got the message loud and clear. He did not want me to say all that "mushy stuff" in front of his classmates and friends. It was like an arrow to the heart, but I understood. I remember feeling the same way at that age. He didn't want to look like a "mama's boy" in front of his friends, and that's fine. So I closed the door to his room, and walked down the hall to leave. As I was opening the door to walk outside, I heard Chad calling me "Mom, wait." He had a hall pass in hand and ran to meet me at the door. He came up and gave me a hug and said "I love you, too... just don't say all that stuff when I am in class, okay?" I agreed not to break the "cool code" again, but was also touched that he did not want me to leave that day with hurt feelings.

Rule nine: New parents (and even some not so new parents) will make at least one of the "freshmen mistakes" of parenting. With five kids, we've made all the freshmen mistakes along the way. There are so many out there, but these are some of the ones that first come to mind. Freshmen mistakes include: Always rocking the baby to sleep, holding the baby constantly, never letting the baby cry it out. Also included are running to the pediatrician's office at the first sign of a sniffle, buying the most expensive diapers/clothes, buying too many presents on the first Christmas/birthday, throwing a big birthday party for a one year old, spending too much money on too many toys, falling for every "must have" educational item to make our children "learn better" (my personal favorite: sight cards for infants... have your infant reading by age one!) Most first time moms sterilize everything of the baby's that hits the ground (most parents don't learn

A View from the Parents' Corner

the "five seconds/blow off the germs rule" until baby number two comes along.... i.e. there's clean and then there's "clean enough") The biggest freshmen mistake of parenting (in my opinion) is putting a baby into bed with you. MISTAKE! MISTAKE! MISTAKE! Once a baby has become used to sleeping next to Mommy — once he has "staked his territory" in the "big bed" — it can take YEARS to get him used to his own bed. The desperation for sleep in those early newborn days is rarely worth the trade off of developing the patterns of light sleep caused by subconscious awareness of having the baby sleeping next to you. And quite frankly, a baby in the grown up bed wreaks havoc on your sex life. (as if parenthood alone doesn't do that enough) This may seem completely unimportant to you in the newborn days, when you can't imagine doing anything with fifteen minutes other than sleeping, but eventually most of us do care about that again. After all, it's what brought you to this parenthood dance in the first place.

There are so many great truths of parenting... things to which all parents can relate. These are just some of my favorites. You can't help but smile when you think of the quirky things that make the interaction between parents and their children so spirited. There is never a dull moment in parenting, and having a sense of humor about it certainly makes the tougher moments easier to handle. But the ultimate great truth about parenting is that no matter how many children you have, each one is an amazing gift, a privilege and an honor to raise. This is a great truth that neither time nor circumstance can ever change.

Primary Colors

"Who we were is not necessarily who we are, but at some point, all children become curious about their parents' lives before they were born."

A View from the Parents' Corner

6. My Mommy Was Famous!

Every child goes through a period of discovery; meaning that he discovers or realizes that his parents were once something other than his parents. We are at that point with our older children. My children are amused to see pictures of their daddy and me when we were dating. David had long, bleached out hair, an earring and played the bass guitar. I was quite smitten with that "bad boy"; in fact, I still am. However, the "boy" in those pictures only vaguely resembles the "corporate" looking Daddy they have always known. My appearance hasn't changed so much... my hair is shorter and I run around without makeup a lot more. Everyone has to (or needs to) grow up sometime, and that happened for us when we became parents. David got a nice "business" haircut and I traded my leather pants for a comfortable pair of jeans. I have a picture of my husband and me above our fireplace that was taken at a spring formal during our freshman year of college. I do remember that couple. We are very different people today, but that youthful glow still exists down deep inside of both of us somewhere. I recently showed this picture to our two year old and he was unable to identify the people in the picture as his daddy and me. Time changes many things, but all of our past experiences influence our present lives in certain ways. Who we were is not necessarily who we are, but at some point all children become curious about their parents lives before they were born.

A long time ago, in a parallel galaxy far, far away... I worked in the radio industry. I started out as a deejay at my college radio station, and through a series of lucky events, soon moved on to bigger things. When I was in my early twenties, before we had children, I worked for three years at a major FM station in Atlanta. I grew up loving music and was even a decent musician myself. However, I knew that my musical abilities were not extraordinary. Working in radio was as close as I would ever get to living out a rock 'n roll fantasy. It was an interesting line of work; a dream job for someone who was young, unfocused, and possessing a head full of foolishness. My job afforded me the perks of meeting famous people, working station promotions at dance clubs, an almost unlimited supply of concert tickets and backstage passes, CD's, and whatever promotional materials record companies provided for us. It was a cushy job, by anyone's standards. The first two years I worked there, I would have moments where I would actually stop and think, "I can't believe I'm getting paid to do this!" However, by the end of the third year, the glitter was wearing off. Everything you hear about the music industry is basically true, and many of the people who work in the business have huge egos and a lot of bad habits, if you know what I mean. By that third year, it was no longer "fun" and I wanted out. It's a very hard business in which to "keep your nose clean". By the time I was married and finished with my undergraduate work in college, I was ready to have a family and I wanted to get as far away from that industry as possible. Fast forward a dozen years...

I've never really talked much about those years with the friends I have made since those days. My friendships that date back to childhood and high school, those people remember those years, but we never talk about it. Life moved on. Everyone who knows me more than casually

A View from the Parents' Corner

is aware of my former line of work. I understand the curiosity people have with it as it is not a typical nine to five job. However, that life is so far removed from the one I have now, it almost seems like a lifetime ago. I would much rather talk about my kids and hear people talk about their kids than to talk about my life before my family.

In May 2004, David and I went to see Rick Springfield in concert. I have to tell you, I REALLY loved Rick when I was a teenager. My mother would not let me go see him in concert when I was growing up; he's one of the few performers I liked growing up that I had never seen live. When I saw an email that he was coming to town, I was so excited. I called my girlfriend, Christina, to see if she and her husband wanted to go, too. After laughing hysterically for probably a full five minutes, she politely declined and accused me of being stuck in the 80's. MOI? STUCK IN THE 80's? Please! Some music is good, regardless of age; and besides, I'm still the coolest mother of five that I know!

Anyway, my husband agreed to go and we had a great time! I have never really gotten over loving to see live performances and that night, I was fourteen years old all over again! I have a confession to make... when we were in our early twenties, David and I saw Elton John and Paul McCartney play live. We just hooted watching all the "old people" (old being 30's and 40's) dancing around, thinking they were still "cool", but in reality were way too old to be acting so ridiculously. All of a sudden, at this Rick Springfield show, we were now a part of that "arthritic, mid-life crisis crowd" or at least in the "too old to rock" group of people. I may have felt fourteen in that moment, but make no mistake, we are most definitely middle aged. Nevertheless, we defied our age that night and had a lot of fun. Even David, who generally likes to "play it cool" and is not overly impressed by anything, thought it was a really good show.

Rick was going to be playing over in Orlando the next night, and I thought it would be fun to take our oldest son, who is just learning to play guitar, to see a live show. We loaded up our conversion van (our very thirty-something mode of transportation) and took the whole crew over to Orlando the next day. On the drive over, we played a Rick Springfield CD, so that Chad would be familiar with the music, and that's when we broke the news that their mommy was once something other than a mommy. I am not sure it had ever occurred to them before. They asked a few questions. But for the most part, they just listened to the CD and enjoyed the ride over.

My husband took our four other children to Downtown Disney while I took Chad to the House of Blues to see the show. We arrived well ahead of show time and stood outside in line, waiting to go in. A security person from the House of Blues was walking through the line, attaching wristbands on to everyone over the age of twenty one. I do not drink alcohol and had no plans to drink that night. However I did put my wrist out as the man approached Chad and me. He stopped and asked in all seriousness "Can I see your I.D.?" I laughed for a moment and then realized he wasn't kidding. I pointed to Chad, who's almost as tall as me and said, "This young man here is my son... do you really think I could be under 21?" He looked confused and asked, "So do you need a wristband?" I shook my head no and watched him walk on. Okay, I know he was probably just yanking my chain, but it did feel a tiny bit good to have him imply that I might could

A View from the Parents' Corner

might could pass for less than thirty four.

Once we were inside, we took a spot down next to the stage. The road crew was checking the equipment and I took the opportunity to tell Chad about everything that was likely going on back stage. For three years, I was allowed to run around back stage at various shows and I have to say, David and I have some interesting stories to tell about those days. Some of it, I look back on fondly. I told Chad the first show we ever watched from backstage was an ancient group called "Cheap Trick". Okay, to us they are not ancient, but to my son, who had never even heard of them, they might as well have been around with the dinosaurs. He was slightly interested in what I had to say, but he had his eyes fixated on the guitars on stage. He is really into electric guitars, and I could tell he was anxious to see one played in concert. Just before concert time, I stuffed ear plugs into his ears to protect his hearing. (I may be a "cool mom", but I'm still a conscientious one). The lights went down and a collective scream came up from the semi-drunk, middle aged ladies in the house. Just as Rick was coming out on stage, I turned to take a quick look at Chad and his eyes were as big as saucers. I watched him as he watched Rick pick up his guitar and launch into a 90 minute set. All of a sudden this aging rock star, standing straight over us, had my son's complete attention and it was a treat to watch. I watched Chad sing along to the songs he knew and air guitar to the ones he didn't know. By the time it was over, I knew two things were true... my son was totally sold on playing an electric guitar and he had just had the time of his life.

As we walked out of the show to catch up with the rest of our tribe, he had a million questions... "Did you really used to work backstage at concerts?" "Did you really meet a lot of famous rock stars?" "Were you a famous person?" The question he asked that stopped him in his tracks was an easy one to answer; he asked "Why would you have wanted to quit a job like that?" The answer was simple; I told him "Because I loved being your mommy more." "Really?" he asked. "Yes, really." It was the first time, I think, that my son really internalized that I was something other than a mother at one point in time. I think he was certainly curious about this "other life", but also relieved that I am "just a mommy" now. A few minutes later we caught up with the rest of our family and Chad talked the whole 90 minute ride home about the show.

Later that week, My son Joey and I had dinner with his teacher from school. He had a particularly sweet teacher, that we were both very fond of, and we offered to take her out to thank her for a great school year. We had not been seated for more than five minutes when Joey pipes up and says "Miss Woodsmall, did you know that my mommy used to be famous?" I about choked on the ice cube in my mouth. I did laugh out loud and corrected him. "No, Honey, Mommy's never been famous." "Yes you were," he insisted, "you used to be on the radio." In his mind, anyone that is on television or on the radio must be famous. I explained that yes, I had worked in radio years ago, but that I was never really famous. Regardless, I could see that he was very proud of me and I sat up a little taller in the booth that day. This school year, Joey asked me to come speak to his class on career day and I had a lot of fun talking to his class about how to get a job on the radio and answering all of their questions... "Yes, I did meet Will Smith... No I didn't become friends with the famous people I met... No, I never sang on the radio..."

A View from the Parents' Corner   53

ABOVE: Laura backstage with Curt Smith of Tears For Fears in 1990
BELOW: David and Will Smith at a radio station Halloween party in 1989

He was very proud to have me speak and it made him the BMOC that day.

It is fun to watch the light come on with kids. The realization that Mommy and Daddy weren't always parents is something that is hard for kids to get their hands around. It has only been in the last couple of years that the kids have realized that we have names other than Mommy and Daddy. For a kid to think of his parents as anything else is to take him out of his comfort zone. Even today, my own mother is "Mom". I don't think of her as ever having been a school teacher, much less wearing any of the many other hats she wore. There's a certain amount of emotional comfort with that; maybe we never outgrow it. A friend of mine asked me recently, "Do you ever miss that life, or wonder where it might have taken you if you had not walked away?" In all honesty, I really don't. When I think back on it, I remember the fun things we did, but I don't dwell on it. My life now is so much more fulfilling than it ever was then or ever could have been had I continued down that road. I believe that my role as a mother is exactly where my life was meant to be, and I wouldn't change it if I could. I don't expect that my kids will want to know all about me outside of my role as their mother, and that is fine. My place in the Parents' Corner is the role that has brought me the greatest sense of joy and accomplishment in my life. If they know nothing more about me than that, it will be enough.

7. Sex, Lies, And Not A Videotape In Sight!

Generally, as parents, we anxiously await every new milestone in our children's lives. During the first year, there are so many... the first time he rolls over, the first time he crawls, the first food, first step, first word, and so on and so forth. We practically sleep with the camcorder within reach so as to not miss one major moment. Once our child is out of the infant/toddler stage, there aren't as many milestone moments stacked on top of each other, but there are still many Kodak moments... the first day of school, the first little league game or ballet recital, and may other things along these lines. One milestone in our child's life, however, that had major significance, was not one that we caught on camera, though I am sure that the look on my face was priceless as I plowed through the discussion on the birds and the bees.

When my oldest son was nine and a half, I was really pregnant, I mean "swallowed a basketball" pregnant with our fifth child. We live five hundred miles away from family, and I had delivered early and quickly with all of my babies. Toward the end of my eighth month, I began experiencing visions or premonitions, or maybe it was just pregnancy-induced psychosis about the upcoming delivery. I was afraid, petrified actually, of having to take my four children into the delivery room, if I went into labor before my mother came to town to watch the kids. Looking back now, I can see that was pretty unreasonable given the fact that we have numerous friends that could have (and would have) helped us out in a jam. But all I could picture was four bug-eyed kids staring at their mother with her legs in stirrups and baring the fruit of her loins. Knowing how frightening a sight that could potentially be, I had my kids watch "The Maternity Ward" on the Learning Channel a time or two (or fifty). I wanted to be sure that they understood that yes, there is some pain and some blood, but that in the end, the mother and baby are fine and everyone lives happily ever after... the end.

For the most part, my attempts at pre-emptive education were met with a high degree of disinterest. Thankfully, The Learning Channel blocks out anything resembling genitalia, which left my seven year old son wondering if the baby was coming out through the belly button. (I never really did answer that... asking "who's ready for some popcorn?" diverted him away from his questions- thankfully). But in the last months of my pregnancy, I felt compelled to let our oldest son in on "the secret" of how we all got here. My own mother had a baby when I was fourteen and I remember being harassed at school when word got around. I remember hearing "Ooh, your parents have been 'doing it'!" and "Your parents still have sex?" being thrown around a few times. And yes, the thought of my old parents ('old' meaning mid-thirties, by the way) doing the "down and dirty" was enough to make my fourteen year old stomach turn.

Needless to say, I was quite nervous about approaching this subject with my son. I went out to a bookstore and bought a kid-friendly book on the subject and read about and thought about what I would say for over a week before I summoned the courage to dive in. I felt that, for Chad, knowledge is power, in this area in particular. I thought the likelihood of him being teased about his mother being pregnant for a FIFTH time was high enough to spark this discussion a little earlier than I probably would have otherwise.

On thinking back to my own birds and bees lecture from my mother, it is hard to remember exactly how it went. I remember being quite perturbed that she called me in from playing basketball to have this "little talk". I had no interest in knowing the differences between boys and girls or where babies came from. As far as I was concerned, boys were just those smelly creatures on the other side of the basketball, with whom I had a perverse thrill in mopping up the court. I was quite a tom boy, very good at sports, and at the age of ten or so, had zero interest in this sex stuff. Of course, by fourteen, I had gone through puberty and had a lot less interest in beating those boys on the basketball court. I was wishing I had paid more attention to "that little lecture" from a few years back. Under no circumstances would I go back to my mother at that point and say "By the way... could you give me a brief synopsis of that sex stuff again?" The response I feared most would have been "Why do you want to know?" We just couldn't go there, if you know what I mean. Okay, fast forward twenty-something years, back to our nine year old son...

I thought of so many profound and thought-provoking things to say to him. I took this as a grand opportunity to show Chad that there was no subject "off the table" between us... that we could talk about anything. We would bond over it, I was sure. If not, there was a strong likelihood that I would just die of embarrassment. Nevertheless, on that fateful Saturday morning, I pulled my son away from the Power Rangers on TV and made camp with him on my bed, at the far end of the house, well out of the ear shot of the other kids.

I had a well-thought out speech in mind. First I'd give him a lesson in physiology-the structural differences between boys and girls, then slip into a brief overview of puberty; then we'd get down to the heart of the matter... what sex is and isn't. It only took about thirty seconds of staring into Chad's face to know that I really should have written a few things down on notecards, because I was all over the place in my talk and was beginning to get diarrhea of the mouth. I could tell by the look on his face that this was "way too much information". I'd pause briefly to ask if he understood what I was saying and to catch my breath, because my mouth was running a verbal marathon.

Overall, the talk lasted just under an hour. I think I took the very long road in driving home the concepts about sex that are both very simple in some ways, but so complex in others. The things I wanted him to walk away with that day were that in a few years he would be undergoing physical changes that would bring him to the threshold of adulthood, and that as much as I love him being a child, I am excited to think about the man he will become. He needed to understand that his feelings about himself, his world, and "gross girls" would change as well, and these were not things to fear, but things to look forward to. I still couldn't convince him that one day he would like a girl that isn't a member of his family, but that will come soon enough, anyway.

In regards to sex itself, I wanted him to know that he would hear a lot of "junk" about it over the next few years, and flat out lies... that people will cheapen it when they talk about it. I wanted him to know that there is a profound difference between the physical act of having sex and making love with someone; the difference has

A View from the Parents' Corner

everything to do with love, commitment, responsibility, and morality. The most intimate form of human contact and the most intense physical expression of love isn't something to be taken lightly. From this very act, human life can be created and that is an amazing thing.

After this, I wrapped up the discussion by saying "And this is how you came into this world, and this is how we made your new sister who will be arriving soon. Do you have any questions?" My son just looked at me and my huge belly for a moment and asked "So that's what you and Daddy do?" I sheepishly answered "Yes" and then justified it by re-iterating (or more truthfully, rambling on some more) about the fact that sex is a very normal, very healthy part of marriage. Mommy and Daddy love each other greatly, and would be only with each other for their whole lives... and it was nothing to be embarrassed about (though I am sure that my beet-red face told a different story about embarrassment). Mercifully, that was the extent of his questions; except for asking if he could go back and watch cartoons. Though it had been an intense, nerve-racking discussion, I walked away feeling pretty good about it. At least I knew that I had armed my son with the correct information he needed about a subject he was soon to hear a lot about.

The only downside to this discussion was the fact that David and I can't flirt with each other over Chad's head anymore. He knows exactly why Mommy calls Daddy "a studmuffin" and that when Daddy says that Mommy looks "hot", it has nothing to do with perspiration. Oh well, I guess we will have to learn to be more covert. Anyway, I know that he will need follow-up, "not so vanilla" discussions as the years pass, and he will probably prefer to have these discussions with his dad as he gets older. I am glad I had the opportunity to have the first discussion. I hope that he will remember that there is nothing he can't talk to me about... because of what we accomplished together on that day.

8. The Alphabetical List Of Dirty Words

One of the wonderful things about children is the innocence with which they approach everything. The purity of heart and in spirit makes them so charming and triggers an instinct in us, as parents, to protect and preserve their innocence for as long as possible. We strive to keep the ugliness and perversion of some aspects of the world from reaching out and touching their lives too soon. The first time our children come home uttering a "new word" they have picked up on the playground, our hearts sink and we know that it won't be long before we can no longer keep the world out. The week after I had the talk with Chad about "the birds and the bees", he came home from school and asked me to come into his room and shut the door. "Mom," he said, "what does a-s-s mean?"

In a calm, unrattled manner, I simply asked him "Where did you hear that?" "It was written on the side of the school building," he replied. Apparently, Chad and a few of his friends had noted it in the carpool line. "Well..." I said. "It actually is a word that means a donkey, but when people say it in a mean way or write it on the side of a building, they mean something ugly by it. It is not a nice word, and if you say it, it will get you in a lot of trouble, especially at school." "I figured it meant something bad," Chad said, "but Joe was teasing me because I didn't know what it meant. He said that I didn't know the meanings of the alphabetical list of dirty words and that he did." Wow! There's a list—excuse me, an ALPHABETICAL list—of dirty words out there?? This was news to me! My son was only nine years old and in third grade at the time, and I thought he was a little young to know about these words.

I don't really remember hearing a lot of bad words when I was growing up until I was in middle school, and even then, I think it was only on the school bus. (a brief footnote about this: every bad thing I ever heard, said, or did, I learned about on the school bus. It is amazing the lessons you can learn on a short ten minute ride to school! Further note: my kids will never ride a bus to school! Back to the story...)

I knew that it was time to lift the veil of innocence from his eyes in this area, to tell him about "the list" for his own protection. I did not want some snotty kid getting my child in trouble by having him repeat a dirty word that my son would utter in innocence, but would get him in trouble, nonetheless. So, on a Saturday morning, a mere week after the historic sex lecture, I again called Chad away from his Saturday morning cartoons and asked him to follow me into my bedroom. "Oh Mom!" he moaned. "You're not going to talk more about where babies come from, are you?" "No, Honey, we are going to talk about the alphabetical list of dirty words you've heard so much about." He seemed relieved, and I felt sick at my stomach. Much like you would if you were getting ready to lick soap scum off of the shower door...I was feeling dirty already. On the way into my room, I spotted our four year old daughter's Magna-Doodle on the floor. "This could come in handy" I thought to myself, and I scooped it up and threw my pen and paper back into a drawer.

There was really no good way to ease into this talk, so the blunt, straightforward approach was the one I took. First, I asked him what words he had heard in the past that he thought might be a problem. Surprisingly, he had not heard anything too vile. We sat across from each other on the bed, "crisscross applesauce". I was armed with Laurie's Magna Doodle, a bazooka load of information and I was ready to get down to business.

"Okay, we might as well start at the top... down the "A-list" I said. Quickly, I scribbled out the word on the Magna Doodle that he had seen written across the building of his school. I gave him all the definitions of the word that I could think of, what it means when used correctly, and what it means when used incorrectly. Then I used the word in a sentence (actually a few sentences) so that he would know how it is used in all senses of the word. Whew! That was tough, let me tell you! He took it all in stride, and slowly we made our way down the alphabetical list. Certain words we took extra time with because of the weight that using those particular words can carry. He did ask very specific questions, and I did answer him truthfully. While we were on this subject anyway, I felt like we might as well cover obscene gestures as well. "What the heck?" I figured. We would be needing a shower after this anyway. I have to admit, at one time, particularly in college and when I was working in radio, I had a bit of a salty tongue. This is not something I'm proud of at all. I had become de-sensitized to it, and found it very easy to use the same gutter language that I was hearing all around me. Eventually, I realized that the people around me I liked the best, the people I thought had the most class, didn't have salty tongues. I now find it to be a real turn off when I hear people use profanity in everyday conversation. It's downright inexcusable when they talk like that in front of children. I have a dear friend, who has a heart of gold and who I think the world of, but when she is upset about something, the things she says can curl my toes. One day I just asked her, "Why do you talk like that? You are so intelligent (she has an MBA in accounting). You're sweet. You have such a good heart. Why would you lower yourself by using gutter language? People who don't know you will immediately write you off when they hear you talk like that." Fortunately, she accepted this line of questioning with the love that was behind it and did not become angry with me. I never really got a concrete answer from her other than it was a habit. And this is the danger in using bad language. It is so easy for it to become a habit and this is something I wanted Chad to understand.

After burning a hole in my daughter's Magna Doodle, and gesturing out the ying yang, I came to what I felt was the end of my lecture. I asked him if he had any questions. He did ask for clarification on a few things, but for the most part he had taken it all in. He asked me why people would ever want to use these words and phrases. "I don't really know." I told him. "Sometimes people say things in anger that they would never say otherwise. Sometimes people talk like that because they want to sound tough. Sometimes there isn't a reason." He just shook his head and didn't really comment any further. But I also told him that there can be a lot of pressure, especially on boys, to "talk tough." But, I warned him, this kind of tough talk could only lead to trouble.

Whenever you arm your kids with this kind of information you hope that you've warned them of the negative implications sternly enough so that you have not opened up a can of worms. Just to insure that he would not take his "new found powers and use them for evil" (could not pass up the superhero illustration, sorry) I warned him that using this kind of language would get him in a lot of trouble at home and at school. In addition, the parents of his friends would not want him to be around their children if he talked that way. Shazaam! Those were the magic words, the words that put fear in his heart! He has a handful of friends he absolutely loves. He couldn't stand the thought of not being able to play with them anymore.

I trust Chad to make good decisions with the information I have given him. In one respect, it felt really good to share this very direct and honest time with my son. In another respect, I felt like I should spray Laurie's Magna Doodle with Lysol and wash my own mouth out with soap. These are not the Kodak moments you picture in your mind when you are cradling that sweet infant in your arms. But there is a sweetness to these moments too. It's touching to watch the trust in the eyes of that child looking to you for honesty; relying on you to give him the tools he will need to grow into a healthy, happy adult someday. The happy days of young childhood with my children are ones I will always treasure in my heart, but I can't really say that I miss them right now. Each stage of their lives is wonderful and I would not go backwards if I could. Watching them grow toward the people they will become is wonderful and exciting, and I intend to enjoy every moment for as long as it lasts.

"...I watched his face fall, and tears well up in his eyes. "So, Santa is not real?" he asked, his voice breaking. My heart sank into my stomach."

9. The Truth About Santa

Being a responsible parent often means having to make the hard calls. This year presented a dilemma I had not anticipated with Chad. At the age of nine, Chad still believed in Santa Claus. David and I decided it was time to tell him the truth about Santa. After all, he knew about sex and "the alphabetical list of dirty words", so I figured it was time to let him in on this one, too.

Truthfully, I had never intended for him to reach the age of nine without knowing the truth. I felt sure that by age seven or eight a classmate at school would spoil the whole Santa thing and he would come to ask me for the truth. I was never going to lie about Santa if he came to me and asked "Mommy, is Santa real?" The thing is, he never asked.

All of our children absolutely adore the holidays. Christmas is a really big deal in our home. We decorate extensively both outside and inside the house. My father accuses us of trying to compete with the Griswald's. We spend days decorating, while Christmas carols blare on the stereo, and we sip hot chocolate in the 80 degree Florida weather. The outside of our house looks like a North Pole village and the inside looks like a winter wonderland. Every year we decorate three indoor trees. A large seven foot pine serves as the "family tree", decorated with ornaments from our travels abroad and the children's ornaments from school, first Christmas's, etc. We have a six foot pink and white tree that is the "girl's tree" decorated with all girl stuff... lace, beads, and porcelain ornaments. A six foot blue and green "boy's tree" is decorated with cowboys, pirates, and sports stuff. It's quite time consuming, this decorating tradition, but everyone participates and it's always a lot of fun. The mood of the holiday is not lost due to the fact that we are preparing our winter wonderland for Christmas while wearing our shorts and flip flops.

The month of December is always anxiously anticipated for its multitude of Christmas parties, city festivals and parades. The holiday specials on television are something that the children love ("Rudolph" being the kids favorite, "It's a Wonderful Life" and "Christmas Vacation" being Mom and Dad's favorites after the kids go to bed.) The highlights of the month are visiting Santa at the mall and preparing a plate of goodies for Santa on Christmas Eve. I don't know how my son made it to third grade without some smart-mouthed kid telling him that Santa was a big lie, but he did. I was dreading telling him the truth. I thought for many days about what I would say, but the truth was not going to be easy to gloss over. "Hey, Honey... you know that little Santa story you've believed since you were in diapers, well, guess what...?"

I called Chad into my room. After all of the heavy discussions we've had in my room, perhaps it should be nicknamed "The bomb shelter". I sat him down and asked him "So what do you know about Santa and how the whole Christmas night thing works?" I was hoping he'd say something like "Oh MOMmmmmm... I haven't really believed in that story for a few years. I was just playing along with it to make you feel good." No such luck. He had no clue about what I was getting ready to say.

I told him "Honey, you are getting to be a big boy and

there is something I need to talk with you about..." and then I told him. He listened closely as I explained the story of Christmas and how the Santa traditions were started and I watched his face fall and tears well-up in his eyes. "So, Santa is not real?" he asked with his voice breaking. My heart sank into my stomach. I wanted to throw my arms around him and tell him "Of course he is real, and we will go sit on his lap until you are middle aged..." But I thought better of it and answered "No, Honey... there is no one man who takes toys all over the world in one night. The image of Santa represents the goodness and selfless giving of Christmas time. But there are no flying reindeer or toy shop or elves. That's just a sweet story that's fun to think about, but it is not real."

Chad just sat there for a few minutes and said nothing. I could see it in his eyes, "How could you lie to me? You are never suppose to lie to me! Have you lied to me about anything else? Can I trust you, Mommy, to tell me the truth?" I felt my own eyes spill over with tears because my words had hurt Chad deeply. His heart was broken and so was mine. I don't think I actually ever lied to my children about Santa. From the time they were babies, we always went to the mall to sit on Santa's lap, with the instructions to tell Santa what you want for Christmas. They watched the Christmas specials like Rudolph and Frosty and never questioned the stories. But a lie through omission is still a lie, and I felt absolutely terrible. It was a very sad moment in my parenting experience. I thought of all the wonderful Christmas seasons of the past and the innocent anticipation of a wonderful person, who comes to your home, knows you by name, and during one special night per year gives you what you hope for the most. I knew that my precious Chad would never feel that same excitement again. I knew he would not listen for the reindeer on the roof or want to leave a plate of cookies for Santa again. The veil of innocence had been lifted and a marker of childhood passed away that day.

After the impact of my words subsided, I could tell that Chad was not only hurt, but angry. "Is there anything else you need to tell me or can I go now?" he asked. I knew that the door had already been kicked open and I needed to walk through it completely. I had just blown a hole in the whole Santa story and things weren't looking too good for the Easter Bunny or the Tooth Fairy, either. I told him those were just sweet stories, too. "Are you kidding me?" he asked, almost crying. I just shook my head no. I put my arm around him to try to comfort him, but he was too hurt and too angry to accept anything from me at that point. "I'm going to tell Joey. He has the right to know." He angrily insisted. "No, Chad." I said. "He's not ready yet. Do not spoil it for him and your siblings. I will be the one to tell them when the time is right." He agreed not to be the bearer of bad news for the rest of our crew and we ended the discussion at that point. I knew he needed some time to think about what we had said and to cool down. I needed some time to regroup. I felt like an absolute heel and at that moment, I wished we had never allowed the whole "Santa thing" into our holiday tradition. But my sweet memories of Christmases when Chad was young were rich with the anticipation of Santa and I wouldn't trade those memories if I could.

Was it wrong to allow my children to believe in a myth, or more harshly, a lie? I don't have a good answer for that. All I know is that in the moment of truth, the "little lie" hurt us both very deeply. My son felt betrayed by his

A View from the Parents' Corner

father and me. Though we had not intentionally let him down, it was a terrible feeling to live with. After Chad walked out of my room, I went into the bathroom and had a good ten minute cry.

After half an hour or so, I went to Chad's room, where he had been since our discussion ended. "You and I need to go out for a little bit and talk." I told him. He hesitated at first (I am sure he was wondering what other bombshells I had planned to unload on him), but then he agreed. We went down the street to get an ice cream (his favorite ice cream) and as he ate, I began to talk. "I felt like you needed to know about Santa now," I began, "because most kids by this age know the truth. I didn't want anyone to make fun of you because you still believed." "Why did you ever let me believe in Santa?" he asked. "Wasn't it fun and magical to believe in him?" I asked him. "Yes.." he answered. "Well..." I said, "Childhood is the one time in life when you can truly believe in what is magical, and that is a special feeling. Unfortunately, when we grow up, we have to let go of that magic a little bit. But the magic of Christmas is not all about Santa and you don't have to give up all of the magic of Christmas, even when you are grown." He continued to listen. "I know you are surprised and disappointed by some of the things I have told you, but it is not going to change one thing about Christmas in our home." I could tell by the softened expression on his face that he was no longer angry. I continued "It would not be possible for one man to take gifts to every child in the world, especially in one night. That's why parents do it for their own children. It is with great love and excitement that your dad and I look for just the right gifts, so that you and your brothers and sisters will have a wonderful Christmas. You will still get the things you ask for, and we will still do all of the fun things that have become our Christmas traditions... none of that will change." "Can we still go to the mall and see Santa?" he asked. "Absolutely!" I said. "You can do that for as many Christmases as you would like to."

He seemed to feel much better after our conversation. "You know," I said, "the greatest gift your dad and I get at Christmas is seeing the joy and excitement you and your brothers and sisters have on Christmas morning. I hope that will not change for you." "I will still be excited." he assured me. I leaned across the table and gave my tender-hearted son a kiss. "I love you with all of my heart, and I will never lie to you again, you have my word." And with that, another milestone with our oldest son was over. There's a certain sadness in surrendering parts of childhood, but I am really enjoying the maturing relationship I have with my son. I know I will have this conversation four more times and it will be tough each time. But for now, I anticipate sharing the holidays with my family with child-like enthusiasm and I hope that my oldest son will do the same.

How Christmas Lives in My Memories: Chad with Santa in 1996

10. Home For The Holidays

On a Saturday morning in October of 2003, I was in the lobby of the dance studio where our daughter takes ballet, waiting impatiently for her class to dismiss. While pacing pointlessly, waiting for time to pass, I noticed a posting on the bulletin board. A drama production company was holding open auditions for a child's part (ages 8-12) in a local Christmas play called "Home For The Holidays." I thought this sounded like a neat opportunity and immediately thought of Chad. Though Chad isn't what I would call overly extroverted, he does have a beautiful voice, and this part called for a child to sing a solo. When I asked Chad if he'd be interested in trying out for the part, I was pleasantly surprised when he said yes. On the day of the auditions, Chad confidently stood in front of the production company and belted out, perfectly in tune, a version of "Silent Night." Joey had gone along with us to the audition and caught the attention of the director's wife. He was too young for the part in the play, but the director walked over and spoke to him briefly, which made Joey feel like he was included.

A few days later, I received a call from the dance choreographer for the show, informing me that Chad had been selected for the part in the play and that they had been so impressed with Joey's enthusiasm and energy that they wanted him to have a walk-on role in the play. Though he would have no speaking lines, he would still be a part of this impressive professional production.

Rehearsals for the show began almost immediately. Chad had quite a few lines to learn, in addition to his solo.

Initially the part called for him to sing "All I want For Christmas Is My Two Front Teeth". The director was going to blacken out his front teeth and make Chad draw attention to his "missing teeth" throughout the song. The problem with that was that he had braces on his teeth and the black out wouldn't work in his mouth. The decision was made three weeks before the show opened to change his solo to "I Saw Mommy Kissing Santa Claus." We must have listened to that song at least a thousand times over the next few weeks.

Those last few weeks were pretty grueling with the rehearsal schedule plus school. As the final days were drawing near, I began to get really nervous. My boys had never been out in front of a large group of people and I didn't know how they would react. It hit me the day of the opening... "What if they have stage fright? What if Chad can't remember his lines, or worse, his song? What if they get out in front of a packed house and freak out? What if I freak out?"

The play took place at the Port Charlotte Cultural Center, which seats around five hundred people. There were to be three shows—one on Friday night and two on Saturday. All three shows were close to sell outs. As I watched the dress rehearsal on Friday afternoon, I thought to myself "I would no more have done this type of thing than I would have cut off my own hand." Growing up, I was good in sports and music and had a lot of self-esteem from excelling in those things. But I was always able to blend into the background. Radio is a perfect job for someone with fear of speaking in front of people... thousands of people hear you, but no one is WATCHING you. I never wanted to be the center of attention and performing on stage in front of hundreds of people would have sent me hurling. When I thought of my son walking to the front of the stage to sing a solo in front of fifteen hundred people over three performances, it made me sweat. Fortunately, neither one of my sons seemed the least bit nervous. I was nervous enough for both of them.

The hours ticked by slowly and I could not eat dinner that night. I was thirty weeks pregnant, nervous and physically miserable as we waited for curtain time. Backstage at any live performance I had ever been to was loud, busy, and basically chaotic. This production was no exception. I watched from behind the curtain as people started filing into the seats as soon as the doors opened, about thirty minutes ahead of show time. "Don't be nervous!" I kept telling the boys. "And if you mess up, just keep going, no one will even notice. You guys are going to do great!" I had more butterflies in my stomach that night than I ever had talking into a radio mic or speaking in front of a group of people.

Five minutes before curtain, the warning lights flashed and everyone rushed to take their places. Still my boys seemed to have nerves of steel. Both Chad and Joey were in the opening scene and I watched them take their places on stage and wait for he curtain to part. Finally the house lights went down and the curtain slowly opened. "Here we go!" I thought to myself. I watched my boys nervously from offstage, looking for any hint of stage fright as they took their first look at the packed house. Still, they looked unphased. Chad made it through his first set of lines without a hitch. I began to feel a bit more relaxed until I heard the intro music to Chad's solo begin. "Come on, baby...nail it!" I whispered out loud. If sheer will could move mountains, then my will would have moved a thousand mountains. I was willing a perfect performance for my son. Chad walked up to the front of the stage and right on cue, broke into "I Saw Mommy Kissing Santa Claus." Watching my baby from offstage... watching his self confidence and poise, made my heart feel like it would burst with pride. As he was approaching the end of the song, a smile broke out across my face that I could not contain, and I have to admit, I started to cry. (just a little) "That's MY boy!" I said to myself.

As the boys exited the stage at the end of the scene, there was only a moment for hugs and congratulations, as the boys had to hurry for a costume change for an upcoming scene. Every thing and every one was moving very quickly back stage, and I hardly had time to enjoy the wonderful job that both boys were doing.

After intermission, both boys were involved in a country Christmas dance number, which I very much wanted to see from the audience's perspective. I made my way into the auditorium and grabbed a stray seat. Both boys did extremely well, but Joey is just a natural born dancer, and his performance in this particular number was outstanding.

Half-way through the number, a couple sitting behind me were talking loudly between themselves. I heard the man say "Look at that little guy in the red plaid shirt... he's really good." The wife replied "Yes, he is... he's cute as a button." I could not resist the urge that overcame me to flash my "proud mama" badge. I turned around and whispered "That's my son! And the boy who sang the solo earlier, he's my son, too!" Both the husband and wife were very sweet and congratulated me on their good job at the end of the number. I'll admit, I brag shamelessly on my kids. I will brag to anyone who will listen. Anyone who knows me even casually knows this. On this night in particular, there was a lot to brag about.

At the end of the ninety minute show, both boys were exhausted, but exuberant. The next two shows went equally as well, and I was so glad that they were able to have that experience. When all three shows were over, the director pulled me over to the side and complimented me on having such well-behaved and well-mannered children. He had never directed a professional production with children, but said his first time with kids was a pleasure. He recommended that Chad have singing lessons to strengthen his voice and highly recommended encouraging Joey, in particular, to pursue theater work. He felt that both boys did very well and that Chad was a natural singer, but also felt that Joey had a lot of natural stage presence and should pursue his talent.

Both boys really enjoyed this introduction to the theater and have expressed interest in studying it further. At some point, I am sure that they will. But the things I wanted most for them to take away from this experience was a boost in self confidence and to learn a lesson about social confidence. (which I believe they achieved) I wanted them to experience the thrill of taking their talents and having the faith and confidence to "just put it out there" and trust that they would be well received in return. That's exactly what happened. When the audience stood and applauded as the cast took their final bow, I knew they were getting something in return for their efforts, far beyond the money they were paid. Their efforts and talents were well-received when they were willing to "put it out there". I hope they will remember the feeling of that applause, and the acceptance that went along with it, in future social situations. I hope they anticipate acceptance and praise from others instead of being fearful of rejection. Teaching a child to have confidence in themselves and their abilities; to just "put it out there" without fear, in a situation where acceptance is not certain, is hard. But I hope they will always remember the feeling of that night, and how it felt to hear that thundering applause that said "well done". I know I always will.

11. Life Is A Beach!

One of the wonderful things about living in Florida is access to the water. I have loved the ocean for as long as I can remember. Some of my happiest childhood memories as a young child center around family trips to Destin with my grandparents and cousins. I do not have many concrete memories of my childhood. However, I have surprisingly vivid recollections of those lazy summer days, spent frolicking on the beach with my sister and cousins, building sand castles, chasing seagulls, and looking for sea shells. Eventually, when I became a teenager, our family quit making trips to the beach. Years would go by and I would look forward to revisiting a place that had been so special to me in my childhood.

When I was pregnant with our third child, David took a job in St. Petersburg, Florida. I must say, I was thrilled to be living only fifteen minutes from the beach. I had every intention, from day one, to give my children the same special memories of wonderful days at the beach that I had. If I had endless amounts of free time, I would choose to take my kids to the beach every day. But life being lived at the hectic pace that it is, we are lucky to make it out there once a week. Let me tell you, it's no easy task to get five kids out to the beach. My kids absolutely HATE putting on sunscreen and cop the old "but I won't get burned" argument every time. My kids, never having been sunburned, have no concept of how painful it can be. We were spending a small fortune in sunscreen, so I decided to invest in UV protected shirts for all five kids. These little numbers were quite expensive, but I surmised that over the course of time they would pay for themselves in what I saved from using less sunscreen. I have to admit, they aren't the most stylish beach wear I've ever seen, (a bright blue, spandex-type material) but good health trumps swanky attire, right? I wish you could see me smirking as I type. These shirts were (and continue to be) even more unpopular than the sunscreen. Without fail, there is a collective moan when I start distributing the shirts, as the kids exit the car at the beach. I am bombarded with "Oh Mom, I don't wanna... why do we haveta?" This is as predictable as the sun rising in the east and setting in the west.

On occasion, I've actually tried to explain my concerns about skin cancer and the pain involved in getting burned. But regardless of what I say, my words are met with a scowl from my older children. If I'm in a good mood I say "Just wear them without complaining and we'll all go for ice cream when we leave the beach." If I am tired or in a bad mood, I'll usually say something along the lines of "Put them on or you're grounded and wipe that nasty look off of your face or I'll wipe it off for you!" Okay, that doesn't happen often, but when it does, it usually means a short outing at the beach. The shirts are not open to negotiation. This is one of those areas where I have to "quit the fun". These shirts are not optional. End of story.

In an act of cosmic revenge or bad karma, I once accidentally left the stack of salty, ocean water-filled shirts in the back of our van for three days in the middle of summer. The van smelled like something had died inside it for days after we extracted the offending shirts. The boys were quick to point out that this would have never happened if I hadn't made them wear the shirts in the first place. I couldn't argue... a spade is a spade. But

A View from the Parents' Corner

nevertheless, the shirts are still an essential element of our beach attire. If you are ever out at one of the beaches in the St Petersburg area and you spot five little folks who look like a cross between a Solid Gold dancer and a Veggie Tales character, then you have probably spotted my tribe.

You can just count on seeing certain things at the beach: sun, sand, waves... and old men in Speedos. Is it just me or is there a disproportionate number of old men wearing skimpy Speedos at the beach? I just want to scream when I see a 70-something year old man in his skimpies. I just want to grab one by his hearing aid and say "Look buddy... there are kids and families at this beach. Nobody, except maybe your wife, wants to see you in "all your glory" any more than we want to see you in a pair of tighty-whities. Put some clothes on! I demand modesty at the beach from my tribe. Everyone else should do the same!

Speaking of modesty, one time I took my kids to a new beach in hopes of finding one less crowded than the one we usually go to. I won't name names, but we found a beautiful and quiet beach on a morning outing, not too long ago. I was quite proud of myself and we made our way toward the water. Out of the corner of my eye, I caught a glimpse of one man photographing another frolicking in the waves. "Hmm, that's strange." I thought to myself. We had been there about five minutes when I noticed an odd number of men hanging out together at the beach, young men wearing little skimpy Speedos. Finally, it dawned on me where we were. We had happened upon a "beach for alternative lifestyles." We were definitely the "fish out of water" at this beach. Not wanting to have to explain that one, I loaded up our beach gear and we headed over to our regular stomping grounds. As I said, "There's always something interesting to see at the beach!"

Our boys are at the age, particularly my oldest son, Chad, when "being cool" is of utmost importance. This is part of the reason he objects so stringently to the sun protection shirts. Part of being cool is not being afraid... of anything. When we go to the beach, both Chad and Joey like to take their boogie boards out into the water and ride the waves back into shore. This always makes me a bit uneasy because of the potential for rip currents, or undertows. When I agreed to buy the boys their boards, it was with the understanding that they MUST wear a life jacket when they ride. This is another one of those rules that can't be negotiated. As the boys have grown older, this rule has become more and more unpopular. In their opinion, the jackets are too bulky and "none of the other kids on the beach have to wear them!" Can you hear the echoes in the wind of my response "I don't care what anyone else on the beach is wearing. You will wear yours and that's final!"

Last summer, several children and adults lost their lives due to rip currents. Of course, children cannot visualize in their minds what it would mean to be put into the middle of a situation where they would be in grave danger of losing their lives. David and I went to great lengths to explain the inherent dangers of playing in the ocean. First, we tackled the issue of undertows. This just blew Joey's mind, who was seven years old at the time. I tried to explain to him that an undertow is a strong current, a great force of water, that is so strong it can pull you under water and carry you out to sea, causing you to drown. I explained that IF they were wearing life jackets, even if they were pulled out to sea, they would not be pulled

A View from the Parents' Corner

under, therefore they could be rescued. Chad asked a few questions and seemed satisfied that, indeed, a life jacket was necessary and we've had little argument from him since. However, Joey just sat there silently for a moment, with a look of deep concern on his face. Finally, he broke his silence and asked, "So, is it like an evil, magic force that reaches up from under the water and pulls you under by your toes? Is that what an underTOE is?" I can only imagine the visual picture that must have been spinning around in his creative little head. Perhaps he was picturing a set of magical watery hands that reaches up to the surface of the water, ready to grab the feet of any little boy who dares to put his big toes in the water! It is hard to not double over with a belly laugh when Joey comes up with things like this (which happens often... he has a wonderful imagination). He was asking this in all seriousness, so I managed to crack only a small grin as I further explained about rip currents and water safety. It didn't take long for him to understand.

Another issue of concern in regards to water safety in the ocean is... well, it's sharks. Okay, I know the probability of getting struck by lightning is much higher than the probability of getting attacked by a shark. But the waters of Tampa Bay are FULL of sharks and I am not taking any chances with my kids. I never like them to go out into the water any deeper than their knees... another rule that is not very popular. My son came home from school one day, fresh from a science lesson on sharks. "Did you know that there are almost three hundred different kinds of sharks?" he asked me. "Uh huh." I said. "Did you know that most of them are harmless to man?" he further asked. "Uh huh." I responded again. "Then why are you so worried about sharks when we are at the beach?" I looked him

squarely in the eyes and uttered one word. "JAWS!"
Of course, he had no clue what in the world I was talking about. So I explained to him about this movie and man-eating sharks and how it had spooked me into quitting surfing when I was a teenager. Immediately, Chad professed that he was old enough to watch this movie and he wanted to see it right away. Of course, we felt that he was way too young to see this movie. I am thirty four years old and I am not sure that I am old enough to watch it again. But this became almost an obsession for him. He talked about it and asked if he could watch it almost daily for a few weeks. Both of the boys think they are old enough to do everything. "I won't get scared", "I won't get hurt", and "I can do it by myself" are the most commonly used phases in my house. But as the gatekeeper of not only their physical health but also of their mental and emotional well-being, I felt I needed to keep this shark and every other scary creature out of their thoughts and out of their dreams. My boys were really making me out to be the bad guy here... "I am old enough, I won't get scared, why are you treating me like a baby?"

I relented and allowed my boys to watch the first fifteen minutes of the movie (the television version, not the theatrical version). Joey barely made it through the opening credits before he excused himself from the room. Chad was a little more resolved. "I am not scared" he said three or four times within the first five minutes. "Me thinkest he doth protest too much." I thought to myself. I forewarned him as we approached the scene with the first victim. The slow cello/French horn music that is now so famous began to play... the woman looked around nervously in the dark mirky water... suddenly the woman felt a jerk, then another... then a scream! My son quickly grabbed the remote and turned off the television without seeing even as much as a hint of blood. "I think this may be a little too much for me" he declared. "I think you are right, and I think you have made a good decision to turn it off" I said to him. Ever since then, I've had no issue with the kids wading too far out into the ocean. The knee rule works just fine for them.

I have at least a hundred or more beach stories I could recall in this book and maybe I will recite more of them in later editions. Our family outings at the beach have been some of the happiest days of my life. I think it is so important for children to grow up experiencing the wonders of nature, of the world around them, together as a family. There is never a time that I go to the beach without being awed by the power and the timelessness of the ocean... of it's unmatched beauty in nature. It's where I go for wonderful moments with my family. It's where I go for moments of deep thought, when my heart is troubled, when I am searching for clarity on an issue. When I stand at the point where the water breaks on the sand and I stare out into the horizon, I am always amazed that the Hand that made this awesome sight is the same Hand that made me and guides my life; and I am completely humbled by the fact that He would call me His own.

One of the greatest things to do at the beach is to look for treasure. Though it would be great to find a lost diamond ring or a wad of cash, we usually define treasure as a really beautiful or unusual-looking sea shell. All of the beaches in our area seem to have a wealth of shells, particularly after a storm or first thing in the morning after the tide has come in.

On a November morning recently, Laurie had the day off from school, and we decided to spend the morning at the beach. Because her older brothers were not home that day, we didn't take all of the usual equipment with us... no boogie boards, life vests, Frisbees, etc. All that Laurie and Zach, her two year old brother, wanted to take was one bucket... to collect treasure. This was an especially beautiful day. The temperature was in the upper 70's with a light breeze and not a cloud in sight. The beach was rather deserted that day since this was the off season here. I immediately noticed as we walked from the car onto the beach that there was an unusual number of shells that day... large and beautiful. I asked my kids if they wanted to walk down the beach and collect the pretty ones. They happily complied and began skipping ahead of me and our infant daughter, Lanie. I noticed that Laurie was collecting every large shell she passed. I cautioned her only to collect the ones that were not broken. Just because they were big did not mean they belonged in the bucket. But being 5 years old, she couldn't resist any shell that she passed.

We had walked probably half a mile down the beach, and turn around to start walking back in the direction of the car. "Mommy," my daughter Laurie said, "Can you carry the bucket? It is getting too heavy for me." I told her that

A View from the Parents' Corner

I could not carry it for her. I was carrying her eight month old sister in my arms and could not carry her bucket, too. "Why don't you look through your shells?" I suggested. "There are probably some broken ones in there you could throw out". Laurie didn't like this idea at all. "But I want to keep all of them." I told her that she could, but only if SHE could carry the bucket all the way back to the car.

As we walked, we spotted a small patch of shells that we had somehow failed to see on our walk up the beach. Now this little area really was full of treasures. There were several big shells that were nearly perfect... no holes, no broken edges and beautiful with color. There were also several small shells that, while far less impressive in size, were just stunning in shape and color and perfectly sized for necklace-making. Laurie and her brother Zach scooped up the loot eagerly and piled everything on top of an already full bucket. This time, when Laurie tried to pick up the bucket, she had to concede that it was way too full and far too heavy. "Mommy! Could you PLEASE carry the bucket?" she asked with an urgency in her voice. "I am sorry, honey" I said. "But if I try to carry the bucket, it might cause me to drop your sister and she could get hurt very badly. You need to carry your own bucket." She set the bucket down on the beach and had a very concerned look on her face. Finally, after thinking for a moment, she said. "Mommy, will you help me go through my bucket and throw away the bad ones?" "Sure" I said, and all four of us sat down of the beach and poured out the contents of the bucket.

Sure enough, her bucket was just full of shells that were big, and certainly at one time had been beautiful, but were now full of holes and broken edges. I picked up one of the shells and showed Laurie why it was not worth keeping. Within a minute, she was happily sorting through the shells on her own, pitching aside the "bad" ones onto the sand and placing the beautiful ones back into the bucket. I only had to show her once what a less than perfect shell looked like. Once she could recognize on her own what a "bad" shell looked like, she didn't need me to point it out to her. She was able to weed them out on her own. After she was through, she and Zach had a marvelous time throwing all of the discarded shells back into the ocean. I think Zach may have actually thrown one the farthest.

I began thinking as I watched the children throw these shells back into the sea that this was a poignant lesson about life, as well. Sometimes, in our daily lives, we can fill our buckets to the top with things that are broken, things that no longer work in our lives... certain relationships/friendships, perhaps career paths, any situation, really, in which we fill up our time, but are not fulfilled in the process. Laurie was content to fill her bucket up with any shell that was big... it didn't matter if it was broken or ugly. She was more than willing to "make do" with these pretend treasures because she wanted SOMETHING in her bucket. The problem was that by the time she came across a REAL treasure, there was no room for it. Why do we fill our lives with things that are broken? Why do we hold on to things in our lives that ultimately will not bring us joy? Why do we "make do" with what we have instead of looking for those rare treasures in life that will make us truly happy? Is it really better to be filled up with something, anything, even if it's broken? I don't think so.

Broken treasure is really nothing more than junk. When

A View from the Parents' Corner

we carry a lot of "junk" around in our lives, the weight of it can cause us to stumble and fall. We must be strong enough, we must be willing to let those things go, even if it means not being filled for a period of time, in order to ultimately find those treasures that will make us happy, that will make our lives whole. This happens in our everyday lives. It's so easy to fall into that trap. Our days can be so full that it leaves no room for the beautiful things in our lives... our children, our spouses, our extended families, our true friends. It's alarming how well we can learn to function without real treasures in our lives. It's amazing how we can fill our lives up with things that are so empty.

After tossing all of the discarded shells back into the water, Laurie retrieved her bucket, which was now much lighter, and we continued our walk down the beach. Ahead of us on the beach was a flock of seagulls, just milling around. This sight was more temptation than my little Zach could stand. Immediately he took off, determined to catch one of those birds. I've always enjoyed watching my kids do this, watching their faces light up with excitement, hearing their voices giggling with delight. Sea-gull catching, of course, is a fruitless mission. Zach was never going to catch one of these birds, but he couldn't care less! The thrill is in the chase, and for him, that is all that it has to be. I thought about what a good lesson this was as well. Sometimes in pursuing a dream, success isn't always about whether or not you achieve the ultimate goal. Sometimes just the pursuit is where the joy lies. The path we choose in life, the goals we set for ourselves, should be ones in which the journey TOWARD the goal is rewarding. The end result shouldn't be the place where we find the joy. The reason for this is simple. We often do not reach the ultimate end goal. Changes in life, changes in the circumstances in our lives often require us to either deviate from our goals or abandon them all together. If the journey toward the goal has been full of happiness and pleasure, we will probably still view the pursuits as having been worthwhile. If we haven't found the journey to be worthwhile, then we can feel like failures. How much happier our lives could be if we chased life like my beautiful Zach chased those birds... with a heart full of joy and without fear of failure!

By the time we walked back to the car, all three of the children (and their mother) were exhausted. Laurie happily looked through her shell collection, while Zach and Lanie fell asleep on the fifteen minute trip home. In those quiet moments, I marveled at the lessons I had learned from my children that day and wondered what lessons I had missed in the past by not looking at life with a child's-eye view. It's a shame that we often lose the ability to see the simple pleasures, and sometimes the beautiful treasures, that life holds for us, if only we would take the time to look.

12. The Miracle

My hardest day as a parent is not a story laced with funny one-liners and a tongue-in-cheek recount of events. My hardest day as a parent was also the hardest day of my life. January 15, 1997, began as a routine day. It was a brisk, sunny January morning in Atlanta, and I was staying at my parents' home with my two sons, Chad, who was two and a half, and Joey, who was eight months old. We were getting ready to move to Heidelberg, Germany, for a year. Our house in Atlanta was sold. Almost everything we owned was in storage, and I was staying with my family while David was attending a business conference in downtown Atlanta. I had fed the boys breakfast early that morning and my mother had volunteered to watch Joey while I took Chad to the park for some one-on-one time. Chad and I had a fabulous time together and we both came home feeling so happy. Joey was still down for his morning nap, so I hopped in the shower and cleaned up for the day. As I was getting out of the shower, I heard Joey waking up from his nap. I quickly toweled off, combed through my wet hair, and put on some sweats and a pair of socks, since it was rather chilly in my parents' home.

After retrieving Joey from his bed, I made my way down the hall. I was going down to the kitchen to warm up a bottle of breast milk that I had pumped for him earlier. My parents had just had new carpet put down on the second floor of their home and on the stairs. It was a very thick, nice carpet that did not hug well to the shape of the stairs yet. I stood at the top of the stairs, took one step down, and my sock slipped on the edge of the next step.

I lost my balance while I was carrying Joey downstairs. Because I was holding on to him, I could not catch myself to break the fall. I ended up going all the way down the entire flight of stairs on my back and ended up at the bottom of the stairs headfirst. I knew immediately that I had broken a bone in my left foot... the pain was shooting through it unmercifully. I only had time to note this for a moment — I was more concerned about Joey. Joey was crying, but there was something in his cry that was very wrong. I had never heard a child cry like this before. My parents had heard the crash at the bottom of the stairs and came running. "What happened? Did you drop Joey?" they asked. "No!" I said "He never left my arms." They knew something was very wrong, too. I immediately got on the phone to his pediatrician's office. They asked me as well if I had dropped Joey during the fall. "No!" I said "He never left my arms." Because I was the one that actually fell, they did not think it warranted me calling an ambulance, but they instructed me to immediately bring him to the triage facility about fifteen minutes from my parents' home.

My mother drove as I sat in the back with Joey, who was still crying this awful cry. I was starting to get very scared. I limped into the facility and upon a brief examination, they took us immediately to x-ray, where the Head of Pediatrics for all of Kaiser Permanente in Atlanta met us. "Mrs. Hull" he began. " We are just going to start x-raying from the head down. We know something is wrong, but we just don't know where." I signed the "consent to treat" forms and my son was strapped on the x-ray table. They took the first set of films and went to the back to develop them. My mother and I sat and waited for them to come back. I began to cry. "What could be wrong with

A View from the Parents' Corner

him, Mom?" I asked. "He never left my arms." Minutes passed, long minutes and I knew that something must be wrong. After what seemed like an eternity, the doctor returned along with two nurses and two paramedics. "Mrs. Hull" he began grimly, "Your son's neck is broken; we need to transport him immediately to Scottish Rite Children's hospital. We've called to alert them that your son is on the way by ambulance." The two paramedics moved quickly to put a neck brace on Joey, who was still wailing. I was shocked as I felt the world collapsing around me. I was unprepared for the words he had just uttered and I completely fell apart. I doubled over in the wheelchair I was sitting in and just screamed. My screaming soon gave way to sobs, as my mother came over to hold me up. "Oh dear God, what have I done?" I kept repeating over and over. I told my mother to call my dad and have him find David at the conference downtown. I had no idea how to get in touch with him. My mother left the room and one of the nurses came over, put her arms around me and just held me while I sobbed. Tears spilled over her eyes too, as she watched a tiny baby, whose life was in peril and a mother who was crying out to God in anguish. "They will do everything they can to help your son" she reassured me. Through my tears, I was watching the paramedics prepping my baby for the long ride downtown. I ached to hold him... to make this all go away. The power to help him was out of my control and it was killing me inside. I was the one who deserved to be strapped on that board; my fear for him and my feelings of guilt and sorrow were almost more than I could bare. "How could his neck be broken? It can't be true." I kept saying. "He never left my arms."

When the ambulance was ready to leave, they wheeled

me over to it, and I sent my mother ahead in her own car, to meet us at the trauma center. Once we were in the ambulance, they kept trying to start an I.V. line in Joey, but his veins were so small they finally had to start it in his head. The paramedics asked me what had happened. I felt so stupid and so responsible. If something tragic happened to Joey, the blame laid squarely with me.

We had driven only a very short distance when the ambulance pulled over into a field. "What is happening? What are we doing?" I asked. But then I heard it. A helicopter was heading toward the field... it was Lifeflight. "Mrs. Hull" one of the paramedics said. "It is critical with neck and spinal injuries that a patient is treated during the golden first hour. This is when the prognosis for recovery is best. Traffic is so heavy, we need to fly him in." I agreed and watched as they unloaded my son and moved him to the helicopter. I limped over to one of the two doctors who had come on the helicopter and that's when she told me I could not ride with him. "Please, please, don't leave without me... don't separate us. Please don't take my son without me!" I pleaded through my tears. The doctor was very compassionate and explained that there was no room for me; that both doctors needed to treat Joey while in flight, and that I would have to get to the hospital by car. "But I don't have a car!" I cried. "I rode over with my mother and she has already gone to the hospital. I have no way to get there. Please don't leave me here, PLEASE!" I begged. The doctor asked me to please try to get a hold of my emotions. Joey needed me to be strong for him and they didn't want to have to sedate me.

One of the paramedics from the ambulance overheard our conversation. "Mrs. Hull" he said. "I am just getting off

A View from the Parents' Corner

duty. I would be happy to drive you there in my car" he offered. Normally, I would never accept a ride anywhere from a man I didn't know. But I was desperate to meet that helicopter at the hospital, so I accepted. I watched as they closed the doors on the helicopter and the engine fired up. I watched the helicopter, with my precious Joey inside, rise into the sky and leave without me. It was the sickest, saddest feeling I have ever felt in my life. I was terrified and felt completely, utterly, alone... I literally fell to my knees in that field, doubled over and just wept. The paramedic came over, knelt beside me, put his hand gently on my shoulder and said softly "I am sure your son will be alright, ma'am. They are going to take good care of him. I'm ready to go when you are." It took almost an hour to get to the hospital by car. During the entire ride, I sobbed and prayed openly. I prayed like I had never prayed for anything before. "Dear God, please help my son; I will do anything, dear God, just please save him." The man I was riding with was trying to be comforting, but I was inconsolable. All I kept seeing in my mind was that helicopter taking off and the words "broken neck" were ringing in my head. If I had put my child in a wheelchair or worse, I wouldn't have been able to live with it.

My husband arrived at the trauma center about the same time I did. My dad had managed to get word to the people running the conference that his wife and son had been in an accident and that his son was being airlifted to Scottish Rite. He didn't know any details until arriving at the hospital. I can only imagine the panic he must have felt when he got that message.

The helicopter arrived at Scottish Rite about forty minutes ahead of me, and I had already signed consent forms when

Lifeflight arrived, so they were already working on Joey when we arrived. I asked my mother to call the church and alert the prayer chain that we were in the middle of a crisis and needed help. A prayer chain is when one person calls a friend to pray, who calls another friend to pray and it continues until everyone in the congregation has been notified. Immediately widespread prayers began on Joey's behalf. We sat next to him in the trauma room, while a team of doctors evaluated him. His x-rays had flown with him in the helicopter and were now being evaluated, since they considered him to be "stable' at the moment. Again, I was questioned about what had happened and I felt like a rotten mother as I recounted the details of the accident.

Before I go any further in the story, I'd like to remind you that the title of this chapter is called "The Miracle" and this is the part of the story where the chapter gets its name. The trauma team took another series of x-rays on my son's neck. This time, the films revealed something very different... his neck was not broken. "How do you explain this?" we asked in amazement. The doctor held up the first x-ray and then the second and said "all I can say is that it is an abnormal finding on a normal child" and that was all he would say about this startling difference. I felt that my heart might burst with love and relief. Joey had actually sustained a break in his left leg as a result of the impact against me as I was falling, but no traces of his neck injury could be found. The Head of Pediatrics for Kaiser/Atlanta, who had originally seen Joey, called me the next day and said that in all of his years of practice, he had never heard of a condition like Joey's. He had no explanation for what he had seen. I have a pretty good explanation; it's called "the answer to a prayer" or in our case, an answer to many prayers. I have no doubt in my

A View from the Parents' Corner

mind that God heard the many prayers going up on Joey's behalf and he chose to intervene. It was a miracle. To call it anything less would be to shortchange God's power and His answer to our prayers. How weak is our faith if we fervently pray to God about something, and then act surprised when he answers our prayers? God looked down at a precious little boy who badly needed a miracle, and on a mother, weeping in a field, whose spirit was broken, and He provided a miracle. No one will ever be able to convince me otherwise.

I admit, I grew up attending church regularly. But by the time I was grown, I was mostly just a Sunday morning pew warmer. This experience brought home to me that God works actively in our lives. I found a new level of faith that I wouldn't have imagined that I could achieve. I will never be the type of person who will beat you over the head with my religious beliefs, but my faith is deeply rooted and I would never try to hide "the miracle" that God demonstrated in our lives that day.

I have thought about this experience so many times from the Parents' Corner. For years I could not re-tell this story without tears welling up in my eyes. It's every parent's worst nightmare to think that something tragic could happen to his child. This is the only time in my years as a parent that I ever questioned my parenting ability. It is the only time in my adult life that I have ever cried in public. I had a deep sense that I had not protected my son from harm, and that I had failed him on a grand scale. It took me a long time to be able to forgive myself for what happened. Joey has no memories of our accident and shows no permanent sign of it. I finally got to the point where I had to let this go, or I'd never be able to have complete confidence in my parenting skills again. I think as parents we have to accept the fact that we aren't perfect in our job every time, and that's okay. But we need to pursue excellence in this area. Most mistakes won't have the grave consequences that this one almost had. My darkest day as a parent ended up being a turning point in my life as far as my faith is concerned. I think this, in turn, has made me a better parent in many respects. I am always mindful that life can be changed forever in the blink of an eye and that joy can be, and should be, extracted from every moment of "just plain ol' normalcy." We don't have to strive to grab big armfuls of "extraordinary" in our lives. Just being grateful for what is healthy and normal really should be enough.

13. I Can Show You The World – Traveling With Kids

Thinking back on my own childhood, I have wonderful memories of listening to my grandmother tell about her great adventures traveling abroad. Every year my grandmother would take four to six weeks off and take a trip overseas, usually with one of her girlfriends. She went all over Europe, Asia, the Middle East, the Holy Lands, the South Pacific, and on and on. I remember seeing the pictures and slide shows from her trips and being absolutely fascinated with the places she went and the people she met along the way. My grandmother always promised me that she would take me on one of her trips when I graduated from high school. Unfortunately, my grandmother passed away shortly before my sixteenth birthday, so we weren't able to take that trip together. However, the stories I heard about her travels fueled my desire to see the world, and that's exactly what we've done as a family.

In early 1997, David's company offered us the chance to live in Heidelburg, Germany, for a year while he worked in its various European offices. Neither David nor I had been to Europe, so we eagerly accepted the opportunity to explore Europe extensively on someone else's dime. The only apprehension we had about going overseas pertained to our young children. Chad would be turning three shortly and Joey was just barely over a year old. I was a little concerned about the language barrier being a problem and about the quality of healthcare for the children. However, we were assured that the language barrier would not be a problem; even though we did not speak German, most of Europe speaks at least some

English (at least that is what we were told). Healthcare would not be a problem either, we were assured.

It took about a month to pack up our whole lives and put them into storage as we prepared to move to Germany. Meanwhile, I tried to do as much research as I could on the places we would be visiting. Knowing that my grandmother had been to all those places, I wished I could recall more details from the stories of her travels.

The flight from Atlanta to Frankfurt, Germany, was almost nine hours. It was a long haul for the two young, rambunctious boys. As I exited the plane, I nervously scanned the gate area looking for David, who had flown a couple of weeks ahead of us to look for a house. The airport was busy and chaotic. Conversations were buzzing all around me, but I couldn't understand anyone. I looked at the signs around the airport, but couldn't read any of them. For the first time in my life, I knew what it must feel like to be illiterate. It's a helpless feeling. I clutched my two boys in my arms and grabbed the diaper bag, and followed the herd of people to where I hoped I would find baggage claim, and David.

After proceeding through customs and having our passports stamped, I finally saw David. It was such a relief to finally be together as a family again. He had found us a rental house in Elsenz, a town about twenty miles outside of Heidelberg. This was a beautiful little town, but definitely "out in the sticks". It only took one day in our new town to see that everyone in Europe does not speak English, and I began to worry.

I'll never forget our first visit into Heidelberg. It was as beautiful as I had imagined it would be. Situated on the Neckar River, the Castle of Heidelberg overlooks the old city, and it resembles something straight out of a fairy tale. "This is going to be an amazing year" I thought to myself.

I found myself making the long trip into Heidelberg everyday with the boys just to have something to do. It was very difficult not being able to communicate effectively with people. Of course, the phone would never ring, and I had no one other than my children to talk to all day until David came home from work. Television and radio was of no use, as everything was in German. Everything had a level of difficulty attached to it that I hadn't anticipated. Even trips to the grocery store were difficult. With all directions on the boxes of food being written in German, I didn't even know how to cook over there. Life in Germany was not going to be as easy as we had hoped.

The local people, for the most part, were not very helpful. There is still quite a bit of Anti-American sentiment in Germany, and a strong resentment from the locals over our military bases being maintained there. We were not prepared for the hostility we sometimes encountered. Once I took our boys into a little shop in the old city to buy a Christmas ornament. The shop keeper literally turned her back on me, and in broken English, said that she refused to serve Americans. She asked me to leave. I was shocked that someone would have been so openly hostile in front of young children. This wasn't the only time that things like this happened. Certainly, there were some Germans who were pleasant and helpful, but I finally got to the point where I began to look for U.S. military people walking in town if I needed directions or help with anything. I found that I could spot an American pretty easily by looking at their sneakers. Anytime I heard "good English" being spoken in a crowded store, I would turn to find that person and introduce myself. Fortunately, we met a nice military family who had two boys around the same ages as ours, and they helped us out a great deal while we lived there.

David was not crazy about the people he worked with in his office. He called them all "trolls". Chad would later announce to his pre-school class once we returned to the U.S. that his daddy had worked with trolls while we lived in Germany. That was embarrassing to have to explain to his teacher. A personal incident with a couple of trolls myself left us all feeling disdain for our experiences in Germany.

About two weeks after our arrival, I had driven into town with the boys to have lunch with David, not far from his office. The restaurant we went to didn't take credit cards, so we had to pool our money to pay the check. This left me completely without cash. After lunch, I began the twenty mile drive back home and was singing some songs with Chad in the car when a police car pulled up behind me, seemingly out of nowhere, and flashed me to pull over. I looked down at my speedometer and was traveling fifteen kilometers over the speed limit (roughly nine mph over). Two officers stepped out of their car and positioned themselves on either side of my car. I rolled my window down and the officer on the driver's side said something in German, which I could not understand. I told him I could not speak German; he immediately began speaking in surprisingly good English. He demanded to see my driver's license. "You were speeding!" he said rather gruffly as I pulled out my international license, along with my passport. He studied them for what I considered an unusually long time. "Are you visiting?" he asked. "No." I answered. "My family just moved to Elsenz; we will be here for a year." I glanced back in my rear view mirror to check on the boys. Thankfully, they had both fallen asleep in the back seat.

I was startled when the officer at my window demanded to see my U.S. license. "Why?" I asked. "Do it!" he responded in a nasty tone of voice. I began to get nervous. The two officers passed my license between each other and spoke to each other in German. Finally, the officer at my window said "You pay me seventy-five Marks, I will let you go." Seventy five marks at the time was the equivalent to about forty U.S. dollars. I had absolutely no cash at all. I had just spent all the money I had at lunch. "I don't have any money" I told him. "I just went to lunch with my husband and I used all of my money. Couldn't you just write me a ticket?" Again the officers talked among themselves. "Then give me a gold watch or something... maybe your ring" he said as he pointed to my wedding band. At this point I was really nervous. I could see that these cops wanted a payoff of some kind, and the defiant side of me wanted to say "You will have to pry this ring off of my cold, dead hand..." But my children were in the backseat asleep and I was becoming frightened; frightened more for them than for myself. "Please don't take this" I said. "It's my wedding ring."

At this point, the other officer opened the passenger door of my car and got in. He searched my car and through my backpack looking for anything of value. But I had nothing. The first officer, still holding my passport and U.S. driver's license screamed at me, "You take us to your bank and get the money." I told him that I did not have a bank account. It was only in my husband's name and I did not have access to it. This made him even angrier, "Then you take us to your house and you pay us or you will go to jail." I knew better than to lead these guys to my house. I did not know what their intentions were, but they definitely weren't good.

"Please, just give me a ticket. I don't have anything to give you." I pleaded. "Out of the car!" he screamed at me, "You are coming with us!"

"No, please don't do this!" I begged. "I've got two babies in the back seat..." But he cut me off cold. "Get out now!" he screamed. The officer by the passenger window said something to his partner I couldn't understand and the two men began to converse. By this point I was visibly shaking. I was out in the middle of nowhere; nothing but fields for as far as the eye could see. I had not seen a car pass by in the ten minutes I had been stopped and I was in the presence of two men with guns and bad intentions. My mind was racing. I was praying in my mind "Dear God, help us. Please don't let them hurt my kids, please don't let them do anything to me in front of my kids, help us." In that moment, they had all of the power and I felt so inadequate to protect my children. I only remember being fearful for my own safety one other time in my life; this was worse because I feared for the safety of my children. I began to think about what I would do if I had to physically defend my children or myself and I knew that we were trapped. Then it hit me.

"I know where I can get you money." I said. "If you

follow me back to my husband's office, he will give you cash." The two men talked to each other (in German, of course) and then agreed to follow me back to David's work, about ten miles away.

When I finally started the car and pulled out onto the road, my dark sunglasses were the only things even slightly concealing the fact that I was shaking and crying so hard that it was difficult to drive.

I looked back in my rearview mirror to glance at my boys, but could also see the officers sitting right on my tail. "Pull it together" I kept telling myself. There was no way I wanted those two men to see how frightened I was. As soon as I pulled into the parking lot of my husband's office, I threw the car in park and raced to unstrap both boys from their carseats. I picked both of them up in my arms and literally ran for the door. I was still shaking when I came to the reception area of David's office and told the lady at the desk that I needed David and every other available man in the office to come outside and help me. Moments later, my husband and several other German men emerged and I hastily told them what had happened. They all made a beeline to the parking lot to confront the officers. The cops looked shocked when the office doors opened and I walked out surrounded by all of these people. A conversation erupted between the officers and the German workers, and at times, it appeared to be heated. We had no idea what was being said, but the officers finally issued me a speeding ticket and left the property, without collecting a dime or in their case, a mark. This incident had preyed upon every fear I ever had about my ability to protect my children, (and myself, for that matter) and left me rattled for weeks afterwards.

Though I am sure that most German police officers are honest, courteous, and professional, my personal experience was frightening. We were really never able to get "the bad taste" out of our mouths concerning our experiences in Germany, and to this day, I refuse to even fly over German airspace! (no, that is not a joke). This incident made us aware of how vulnerable we were traveling outside of the U.S., particularly with children, and we were on guard from that point forward.

For the most part, our further travels in Europe were wonderful. We spent three absolutely fabulous weeks in London. We stayed in Piccadilly Circus, about two blocks from Buckingham Palace. Everyday the boys and I ate breakfast at the hotel, watched "Teletubbies" on television (a new BBC show, that at the time was only being broadcast in Britain, and I was confident would not be sophisticated enough to EVER make it's way to the U. S. Little did I know that it would be huge in the States a few years later!) Then we'd set out for the day's adventure. First I would load the boys into their double stroller and go watch the Changing of the Guard. Chad absolutely loved the soldiers and we ended up buying him a soldier costume at Harrod's before we left London. On one of David's afternoon's off, he joined us on a tour through Buckingham Palace. We were fortunate to be in London during the short period of time that Buckingham Palace was opened to the public for tours. That was the most amazing place I have ever seen. It's hard to believe that people really live like that. I'm glad that we had the chance to see it, since the Palace is not likely to be re-opened to the public again.

Other places I took the boys included the Tower of London

A View from the Parents' Corner

(the boys really liked the Beefeaters), and to The British Museum, and many other sites around town, (basically, wherever our hearts led us). During one of our visits to the British Museum, the boys and I stopped for lunch in the cafeteria. A woman sitting at the table next to us heard me talking to my boys and recognized my accent. "You're from Georgia, aren't you honey?" she said. I just smiled and said yes. She was from Georgia, too. "I don't know how you manage your way around here with those two young'uns." She said. I heard this more than once when I was out and about with the boys. I took the boys all over London. There was no way I was just going to sit in a hotel room until David came home from work. Seeing London had always been a dream of mine, and I wanted our boys to experience it to the extent that children that young can, and by golly, come hell or high water, "I was agonna do it!" My southern accent got me stopped more than a few times while we were in London. Apparently, southern accents are considered "really cool" over there. I was surprised that the British would know the regional accents in the States, but many of them did!

Toward the end of our stay in London, Princess Diana was killed. Yes, we were in London when Diana died. We woke up early that August morning, turned on the television and there it was. We were shocked. Being in London during that time was a wild experience. The grief that country felt was like none I had ever seen. I still have the morning edition of a London paper announcing her death. Two weeks later, we picked up a copy of the "Candle in the Wind '97" CD single from Harrod's. Today, it still has the Harrod's seal on it... we've never opened it. These will be interesting mementos for the kids when they get older and understand they were present when a piece of history was being made.

While in Europe, we took the kids throughout Germany, along the Romantic highway. We also visited Belgium, Holland, the outskirts of Britain, Austria (the most beautiful place on earth!) and France. One of the best days of my life was a wonderful day we spent with the boys at EuroDisney, outside of Paris. However, the most amazing adventure of our overseas experience took place on a weeklong trip to Egypt. For as long as I could remember, I had always wanted to see Egypt. I remembered that I had seen a picture of my grandmother riding a camel in Egypt, with the great pyramid of Giza in the background. I wanted to do the same thing.

Our trip to Egypt was not part of my husband's work. We took this trip as a family vacation. Originally, when we booked this trip through the German tour office, our trip was suppose to take us to Cairo and then to Jerusalem. However, the week before we were to leave, heavy fighting had broken out in Jerusalem, and it was considered unsafe for Westerners to travel there. We were hastily re-booked for a trip to Cairo, Aswan, and Luxor.

Our four hour flight on Egypt Air from Frankfurt to Cairo was delayed and we ended up arriving in Cairo at three o'clock in the morning. As we approached the door of the plane leading out onto the runway, I was overcome by a stench like I had never smelled before. This stench was so strong that it was actually very hard to breath. "What is that smell?" I asked David. But he didn't know either. As we walked down the flight of stairs onto the runway, the plane was surrounded by Egyptian military carrying machine guns. I thought, "What have we gotten ourselves into?"

Our tour guide spotted us as we made our way to baggage claim and took us to our car that would be transporting us to our hotel. "I'm worried" I whispered to David. "Me, too" he said.

The hotel where we were staying was a five star property. We had been strongly advised to stay at a five star property for the sake of food and water safety. It was a very nice place and once we were in our room, I felt better about the whole thing. A good night of rest was desperately needed and things were sure to look better in the morning.

Our first morning in Egypt was unbelievable. Our first stop of the day was in Memphis, the oldest city in Egypt. I kept telling David "pinch me, I can't believe we are in Egypt!" Our tour guide was very nice and spoke fairly good English. We were the only native English-speaking people on this German tour, so we had a van and a guide all to ourselves.

The second stop of the day was at the Great Sphinx. What an amazing site! It was very easy to get wrapped up in the wonders of the sites we were seeing, and to let our guard down concerning our surroundings. At one point, our guide said "I want to get you out of here. I think a group of men are following us." We hastily made our way to the van and went to our next sight. As we drove down the streets of Cairo, I could see why the air had smelled so strongly the night before. As we pulled up to traffic lights, donkey carts pulled up right next to us, moving along with traffic. Down in the alleyway, piles and piles of rotten garbage were in the streets, where barefoot children were playing and goats were grazing. Both animals and people defecated in the alleyways. This is where the awful stench was coming from. This was definitely a third world county; and we were not prepared for the culture shock.

The final stop that day was at the Pyramid of Giza, one of the seven wonders of the ancient world. It was an amazing sight to behold. I climbed to the top of the pyramid, just to be able to say that I did it. While there, I rode my first camel. I grabbed Chad and we hopped onto a kneeling camel. When that camel stood, it was much higher in the air than I had anticipated. Feeling like we were going to fall, I held on to Chad with one hand and on to the camel, with a death grip, with my other hand. David took a picture of Chad and me on that camel, with the pyramid in the background. In the photograph, you can see the white-knuckle (literally) grip that I had on that camel's saddle. To this day, that's still my all-time favorite snapshot.

As we were walking toward our van, I turned back to take a few more pictures, as David, the kids, and our tour guide kept walking. Three men approached me, and one of the men said in broken English, "My friend wants to marry you." We had been warned prior to our trip that blonde haired/blue eyed people stood out like sore thumbs in Egypt and that we might attract some unwanted attention. I knew the fact that I had light-hair is what had their attention. I just smiled, trying to be polite, but they were making me uncomfortable. Again, the man repeated "My friend wants to marry you." At this point, I turned and said "I am already married and that is my husband." I

A View from the Parents' Corner

began to walk in the direction of my family. The men took a few steps in my direction, but our tour guide walked up to me and the men left. Several times during our week in Egypt groups of mostly women would walk up and want to touch our children and take pictures of them. It is so rare to see blonde haired/blue eyed children in that part of the world. Even though I'm sure these people meant no harm, the excessive attention directed at our children was very unnerving. We didn't consent for them to be photographed or touched. By the third day of the trip, I told the tour director that I was concerned about our safety and wished to return to Germany. I was told there was no way to get off of the tour early. We would have to stay on the planned agenda.

For the most part, the rest of the week went by smoothly. We went into King Tut's tomb in the Valley of the Kings. We toured the Temple of Karnak and many other amazing monuments. As a child who grew up studying about Moses, Rameses the Great and the land of Egypt, it was thrilling to walk in the same sand that these great men had walked in thousands of years ago. The pyramids are awe-inspiring and it is humbling to walk among them. I have so many wonderful photographs of the children at these great sights. Both boys have had chances in school to talk about having been to Egypt and to share pictures from our time there.

During the whole week in Egypt, we were extremely careful about the food we ate. We only drank bottled water and had managed to make it through the whole week without getting stomach sick.. until the last day. We had been on a three day cruise up the Nile when David and Chad woke up sick on the last day. David was sicker than I had ever seen him in the nine years I had known him. Chad was very sick as well. So far, Joey and I seemed fine, but I was worried, particularly about David. I had stomach medicine for the trip, but this was far beyond anything that my medicines would treat. I called the tour director and told him that my husband and son needed to get to a hospital and to get us on the first flight home. He called me back a few minutes later and said he was putting us on a flight back to Cairo. This time I was forceful. "No!" I shouted at him. "Get us back to Germany, today!" Twenty minutes later, a car arrived to take us to the airport and we were on our way back to Germany. David and Chad were so sick that the airline put us up in the first class section, where no one else was sitting, just to keep us separated from the other passengers. It took us six hours to fly home with stopovers, but I was just relieved to be out of Egypt. I called our military friends in Heidelberg and asked them to buy us a truckload of Gatorade from the military PX.

We took Chad to the hospital in Heidelberg. The language barrier was a real problem. They kept telling us that he just had a virus and wouldn't even give him I.V fluids. We couldn't make them understand just how sick he was. They did not run any blood test or take any stool samples. It was so frustrating to be experiencing inadequate healthcare in a time of serious need.

The next day, Joey and I came down with the illness. Fortunately, Joey had a rather mild case of it, but my case was severe. This was the sickest sick I had ever been in my life, hands down. David said the same thing about himself. I finally flew back to the U.S. with the boys to seek medical treatment. The doctors here never really

A View from the Parents' Corner

figured out what we had, but gave us a medicine called "Flagyl" that kills everything in the intestinal tract. Three days after taking this medicine, we were well. Our Egypt experience taught us that there is a whole different level of being sick. Even today, if one of us in our home is starting to feel poorly, Egypt is the barometer by which all other illness are measured... "Are you feeling just sick or are you feeling Egypt sick?"

Our time in Europe left us physically depleted. David and I both came home about ten pounds lighter than when we moved to Germany. After months of excessive physical exertion from touring, and the effects of poor nutrition, due to the very different European diet, we were in bad shape, physically. In the area of Germany that we lived in, if you don't eat sausage or drink beer, you are in a lot of trouble. As a Georgia girl, raised on good southern cooking, the lack of fruits and vegetables available in our area was disappointing. I was NOT going to eat cow tongue, or meat from an animal that could be classified as a pet, or any other strange body part of some unfortunate "Fear Factor" animal. The Germans in that area traditionally have their first beer of the day at 10:00 am. Who could stomach a beer at 10:00 am? We ate oatmeal... lots of oatmeal. Occasionally, we'd pop into a McDonald's, (they really are on every corner, it seems) but with the whole mad cow scare, we were limited to chicken nuggets and fries, which if you are over the age of five, it isn't that appealing. (Just a footnote: For some reason, French fries and ketchup taste different in Europe, I don't know why.)

One thing I was looking forward to the most upon returning to the U.S. permanently was a vegetable dinner.

I called my mother from Germany the day we left and put in a dinner request. As we were taxiing down the runway, all I could think was "in ten hours, I will be back on American soil. I'm coming home (even though we didn't actually have a place to live yet). And I thought "in ten hours, I will be eating steamed carrots, mashed potatoes, yellow squash, broccoli and roast beef." I visualized that dinner in my mind the whole way home, I kid you not. As wonderful as many of our experiences were in Europe, we were really ready to come back home to the United States. Those months in Europe drove home how lucky we are to be Americans.

After moving back to the U.S. we didn't return to Europe until the spring of 2001. During the 2001 trip, we took the kids (Laurie was here by this point) on a month-long run through Switzerland, Austria, Italy, Monaco, and Southern France. This trip was completely amazing from beginning to end. I made the mistake of taking an "Alabama Crimson Tide" sweatshirt with me on this trip. Any experienced traveler knows not to wear any clothing that marks you as an American. I knew that; I just didn't think about it when I was packing for the trip. Imagine my surprise when I heard someone yell out "ROLL TIDE!" in the middle of the Roman Forum. I turned around and was greeted by another American wearing a Crimson Tide hat... small world!

Rome was amazing and Chad and Joey were both old enough to be impressed by the Colosseum. They also thought the Leaning Tower of Pisa was "really cool" and were blown away by the Alps (and seeing snow for the first time they could remember) in Austria. To this day the kids still ask when we can go back to Austria to see snow.

A View from the Parents' Corner

(They don't realize that it snows in some parts of this country too!) It was on this trip that we came home with a wonderful bonus package... Zach. I have never been one to get air sick when we travel. As we flew home from Switzerland, I was experiencing extreme nausea on the last leg of the trip. A week later, I found out I was pregnant. (Venice is a romantic place, what can I say?)

The last big trip we took was in February 2003, when we took our crew for a two week run to Hawaii. (To Oahu, and the Big Island) I am really a Europe fan, so I was not overly thrilled about this trip initially. David had always wanted to go to Hawaii, so this trip was more for him. I figured, "we live in FLORIDA, we can go to the beach here. Why do we need to fly six thousand miles to see a beach?" Boy did I misjudge this place! This trip was every bit as exciting as the ones we had taken to Europe. We chartered a plane to fly us around the big Island and to fly us over the Kilauea volcano, which is still erupting. Our kids got to see humpback whales up close on a whale-watching tour. They were able to see one of the world's only black sand beaches. These are just a few of the many wonderful experiences they had on this marvelous trip.

Admittedly, I am a travel addict. I'm always looking for the next place to visit. Putting a good travel deal in front of me is like sticking a six pack in front of an alcoholic. I consider it a passion, one that my family seems to share. People have often asked me why David and I would want take our children with us on trips of this nature. They are always quick to point out that traveling with children is both difficult and expensive; as if that had never occurred to us. The reason we choose to travel with our children is pretty simple: we just want to. We want them with us when we experience these great things. We are fully aware that they could not possibly appreciate to any large degree at this point what they are seeing and experiencing. Yet, this becomes less and less true as they get older. Someday they will look back at our travels and understand what a gift those experiences were, and hopefully it will mean something to them that we WANTED them with us on our adventures.

We feel it is important to expose children to the wide variety of experiences that extensive traveling provides. Our children have learned from a very early age about the differences in people and places throughout the world; and in some cases, they've seen how much people are the same in a lot of ways.

Traveling with young children isn't easy; make no mistake about that. It means we must move a little slower and hit the "highlights" of the places we visit and not try to do everything that we might have an interest in seeing. It means so much to me that we have seen and experienced so many wonderful things through our travels and that we were able to share that with our children.

I really do believe that the children have benefited in many ways from our travels. Though they probably have only vague memories of living in Europe, I know that they have seen the videos and photographs enough times to keep the memory of being there alive in their minds; particularly in regards to our trip to Egypt.

Both Chad and Joey have recounted our many trips in both book reports and oral reports at school. Joey proudly told his class this year about being at the Colosseum in Rome on his fifth birthday and having his picture made with a "gladiator". Chad told his class about the "canoe" ride he took in Venice when he was almost eight years old (he just can't ever seem to remember the word "gondola"), and about "standing on top of the world" in the Alps of Austria. Last year, Chad gave a whole presentation to his class about our trip to Hawaii. He spoke eloquently about seeing the migration of the humpback whales and flying over an erupting volcano. Can you really put a price tag on experiences like these? No one could ever convince me that we've wasted our time and money taking our children on trips they could not possibly appreciate. They may not "get it" in terms of the whole picture, but the experiences have most certainly been enriching for them.

The bottom line is that we are a family... we do the "big things" together as a family. No one gets left behind, for any reason, regardless of age or ability to "appreciate" the experience. When our fifth child was born, someone asked me if this would slow us down as far as our traveling was concerned. My answer? Probably not. It may be a few years before we return to Europe, as it is not the safest place for Americans right now; and we would never knowingly take our children into a situation that could potentially be unsafe. But there are plenty of places to explore in our own country and we are planning trips to both Washington D.C., and to the Grand Canyon in the near future.

Traveling is so very rewarding for many reasons and it is a pleasure to share the experiences with our children. People have asked me "Why don't you just take these trips one day when the children are grown... it would be easier then." I hope that David and I will have the opportunity to re-visit many of these places someday when the children are grown. But as life can promise us nothing, we take advantage of the opportunities presented today. I want to see the world while we are young and healthy. I want to see the world with my children, and to see it through their eyes, as well as my own. We have the opportunities now... why not seize them? Why avoid it because it won't be easy? Why gamble and wait for another opportunity down the road that might not ever present itself? I get very frustrated with people who refuse to live in today because they are so busy anticipating tomorrow. Tomorrow never comes for some people. Traveling with our children, for me, is a great example of living and feeling life fully. I don't regret one cent or one minute spent doing it.

A View from the Parents' Corner

Mini Travel Photo Album

My all-time favorite picture

ABOVE: Egypt, 1997
BELOW: Chad and Joey with a Beefeater at the Tower of London, 1997

A View from the Parents' Corner 121

ABOVE: Mount Hungerberg, Innsbruck, Austria, 2001
BELOW: The Roman Colosseum, 2001

ABOVE: David and Zach at the Place of Refuge in Hawai'i, 2003
BELOW: Punalu'u Black Sand Beach in Hawai'i, 2003

A View from the Parents' Corner

Orlando is our favorite short-trip destination

"Balance in our homes is what makes it possible to experience joy to the fullest degree in every wonderful experience of our lives."

14. Parenthood: The Great Balancing Act

What is balance? Can it be defined? The question is like asking "What is quality?" I know it when I see it, but it is hard to define or explain. Likewise, I know balance when I see it or am experiencing it, or when sometimes not experiencing it in my life, but defining it... that's a tough one. Does having balance in our lives mean giving equal amounts of time and effort to everything in our lives? Not all things need or demand it. Is achieving balance in our lives more like a juggling act of keeping all things moving in a set way? Some parts of our life are like juggling rubber balls. Drop them and they will bounce. Someone else can usually pick them up. Other balls, however, are glass. Drop them and they will shatter.

Perhaps balance is more like stacking a house of cards, with the fear being that one misplaced card could cause a lack of balance in the structure, thereby causing the whole thing to collapse. What is balance? We must figure out what balance means in our lives and work towards it.

When I first started sketching out what I wanted to say about achieving balance in the home, I was sure this would be the shortest chapter in the book. After all, I am a relative novice in this "balance stuff" myself. I wasn't sure that I could pull from my infinite wisdom (and yes, I am chuckling as I type this) any pointers or light bulb ideas to enlighten my readers. I don't think there are too many universal rules or great truths in regard to this issue. I think it is a "search and find" mission, a quest, if you will, to strike a healthy balance given the demands in our lives.

An important ingredient in being happy, not only in the parenting role, but in life in general, is maintaining balance. This is almost a no-brainer. However, in today's hectic world, maintaining a balance between work and play, job and home, or whatever responsibilities take our time, is very difficult. Before children enter our lives, it's very easy to allow work/careers to throw our lives out of balance. Putting in 60+ hours per week at work leaves little time or energy for leisure activities. People can maintain this type of approach to life only for a certain amount of time before there is significant danger of total burnout. I can testify to this. I still have the singe marks to prove it! Without down time in our lives, the resulting overload of unrelieved stress can make us vulnerable to physical ailments as well as mental and emotional ones.

When time is not given to relationships, it's hard to keep them intact. Friendships are often the first casualty, as unattended friendships tend to drift apart. Marriages left unattended for long periods of time are particularly vulnerable to affairs and divorce. This isn't news. Everyone knows a home that's been sacrificed on the altar of a career. It's always sad to see, particularly with people you care about. Careers aren't the only things that can jeopardize the happiness of the home. It is critical to be able to balance our roles as parents with the roles we also have as spouses, friends, and separate individuals.

This has been a particularly challenging issue for me as a mother of five children. I must admit, for years I had a serious lack of balance in my life. In trying to be "the perfect mom" I was often ignoring that I am still Laura and I wear many different hats... as a wife, mother, daughter, sister, friend, and even occasional writer. The workload

A View from the Parents' Corner

involved in caring for five children and running a home of seven people is, at times, enormous. Learning to balance the workload is critical in not being crushed by it's weight. In a physical sense, parenting is often draining—it leaves you exhausted at the end of each day. At the same time, if your life is in balance, it leaves you happy and ready to do it all again the next day. When life is out of balance, the mental and emotional aspects of parenting can leave you feeling like you are bearing the weight of the entire world on your shoulders and your knees are starting to buckle. That's a dangerous place to be in our parenting experience. Being able to recognize this in our lives is the first step in correcting it.

In April of 2003, David and I planned our first trip away together since we've had children. When we initially started planning our short weekend together in Orlando, I could hardly wait. The thought of being alone with my husband for the first time in nine years was exciting. I actually went out and bought some "un-mom" looking clothes just for our weekend... specifically, shorty shorts and a tank top that would have made my mother blush. David liked the new look and appreciated my efforts on his behalf. But as the time drew near to leave, I felt very torn. Even though I knew that the kids would be fine staying with my parents while we were gone, and that David and I really needed this time together, the mother instinct in me took over and I felt guilty for leaving. The first night in the hotel, I woke up several times, wondering if everything was okay at home. I knew that it was, and that I was being ridiculous, but still, it bothered me. Finally, I was able to sleep, but it was a restless sleep. (Note: This must be a "mother thing", my husband had an annoyingly easy time getting to sleep. Apparently my pacing didn't bother him one iota. At one point I got "nose to nose" with him while he slept thinking that my mere presence would be enough to wake him into suffering with me... no such luck!)

Whenever I recount the story of this particular weekend to a friend, I often start out by saying "I'll never forget waking up that first morning in the hotel with my husband..." This is usually the part of the story where I pause for effect. Inevitably, when I talk about this "incredible" morning I had with my husband, a grin cuts across the face of whomever I am talking to. I am sure they are anticipating some steamy "love in the morning" story, but that is not what was so incredible (sorry Honey, you know what I mean). I remember waking up that morning and thinking to myself "Wow! I don't have to get up and make breakfast for anyone today!" At home, as soon as my eyes open in the morning, my feet hit the floor running, and I run all day until it's time to go back to bed. To wake up slowly in that hotel and not have to get up was an amazing feeling. I remember looking over at my sleeping husband and thinking "How did we go nine years without taking this time for us?"

I didn't realize how much I missed being "David and Laura" because we are so wrapped up in our roles as "Mom and Dad". I remember how good it felt to just hold hands while we were walking around Epcot. When you have five small children, the parents' hands are always holding smaller hands, carrying babies, or pushing strollers. It was during that weekend away that I became aware of how poorly I balanced my roles as a wife and mother. Even though David and I were always together, it was more in our roles as parents than as husband/wife.

And fifteen or twenty minutes of intimate time back in a bedroom a few times per week is not enough time to reconnect as spouses after many more hours relating to each other in the parenting roles. Besides, I do not know of one marriage in my circle of friends whose sex life hasn't taken a beating at the hands of parenthood. When you are too tired both physically and mentally to catch up with each other in the bedroom, there had better be some other connections keeping you together, or it won't be long before the marriage is in serious trouble. That sometime-studmuffin had better also be your best friend, in addition to your parenting partner, or there is a strong likelihood that the marriage won't survive in the long run.

That weekend away with David provided a lot of clarity for me on issues I didn't even know I had. I became aware of how much I still needed David to see me and relate to me as Laura, the girl he fell in love with in college... glimpses of that girl still exist down deep inside. Of course, this desire to have him see me in this light does not take away from me also wanting him to relate to me, and respect me, as his wife and the mother of his children.

Those thirty six hours with my husband were wonderful and much needed. By the end of our trip, we felt rejuvenated and we were both ready to get home; we really, really missed the children. But that weekend showed us how much we needed to be able to balance the roles in our home. We make a point to set aside time regularly just for "us". I know this seems like such a no-brainer, but it's easy to let a lot of time, years even, go by without dealing with each other as spouses, not just co-parents. I need validation in areas outside of my role as a mother. This is part of being in balance for me. I have made more of an effort lately to take time out for my friends and time out for myself in order to relieve some of the stress that comes along with mothering five children. I love my role as a mother and consider it an honor and privilege to raise these wonderful children. But taking some brief time away from this role creates a balance in my life, which I believe makes me a better parent.

Parents aren't the only ones in the household who need to achieve and maintain a sense of balance. It's just as important for children to live balanced lives. Once children become school age, their lives become a sort of balancing act. After spending an average of six to seven hours per day in the classroom, they often spend a few hours in the afternoon in studies, and then spend additional hours in extracurricular activities during the evenings. Often our weeks (and sometimes weekends, too) are so packed full of things we "must" do that it leaves very little time to just "veg". Trying to keep up this kind of pace for long periods of time inevitably leads to burnout. During the couple of seasons that our older boys played baseball, they were always excited when the season began. However, after a couple of months of "living at the ballfield", they were always tired and no longer enthusiastic. Finally, this year we decided to give up on these types of activities; they just don't fit into our lifestyle. Our boys still study karate two days per week, and have recently begun music lessons. That is plenty. I am sure we will add more activities as they get older and show the desire to try other things. However, I'm not going to be the one to over-commit their time. Often as parents, we are so anxious to introduce our children to everything, that we make a freshman mistake. We forget that we can't do everything and we often meet ourselves coming and going at the door when we try. Life is stressful enough without heaping unnecessary commitments of our time on top of it.

In another aspect of balance, children need one-on-one time with their parents. This has been a struggle in our home. With five children, it's hard to give each child individual attention every day. My kids are often grouped together as "the Hull kids" and I am sure that this is true in most other large families as well. For example, people at church don't necessarily know their individual names, but know that "that's one of those kids who belongs to that family of breeders"... and yes, that has actually been said.

The truth is that each one is unique and has different needs. The reality in our home, however, is that there are five of them and only one of me. I make an effort to take each one of them out individually once per week, just to have some one-on-one time. Often, we just go for a milkshake and sit and talk for thirty minutes or so. Sometimes I will take just one of them with me to the grocery store in the early evening. It doesn't usually involve much fanfare, money, or really that much time, but each child needs that time alone with me, and I try my best to give it. Of course, I've always worked with them individually on their homework, and I tuck them into bed every night. I can always tell when one of my kids is needing some extra attention, and I try to address that need promptly.

Recently, I took my five-year old Laurie out of school for the day and we went to Busch Gardens, while my mother was in town visiting. Laurie is the middle child in our home, and with the schedule of our older boys and the demands of two babies younger than her, it's sometimes easy for her to get lost in the shuffle. I have never seen her act blatantly jealous of her siblings, but I do think she gets tired of seeing the younger siblings take the bulk of Mommy's time and attention. Laurie was very happy to see her little brother and sister stay home with Grandma while she had me all to herself. She talked and talked, and smiled and laughed. It was really nice to have this time to focus on Laurie without any interruptions. Of course, these types of days aren't as numerous as I would like, but I try to have days like this with each of my children. It's good for them, and it's good for me, as well. The needs of each individual child are not necessarily met when addressing the needs of the group.

Overall, I think there are many more positive than negative aspects of raising a large family. We have to be very mindful of making sure each child gets the individual attention he/she needs, but children from large families are generally less demanding, more adaptable, and more self-reliant than children from smaller families—not because they are necessarily better kids, but just because they have to be. Maintaining balance in their lives is critical in making a household of our size (and really any size) work.

Sometimes this high-wire balancing act is tricky, and sometimes you feel like you are teetering without a safety net below. But balance in our homes is what makes it possible to experience joy to the fullest degree in every wonderful experience of our lives. Balance and happiness go hand in hand, and it could be argued that you can't have one without the other.

15. The Buck Stops Here: Raising Kids With Good Character

Back in the late 1980's, long before I had children, I was sitting in the waiting room of a doctors office reading a magazine. I came across an article that was recounting an interview with Jackie Kennedy. I have never really been a big fan of the Kennedy clan, but I had always liked Jackie Kennedy for reasons that had nothing to do with politics. Jackie Kennedy rarely granted interviews, so I was very curious about this article. It covered many topics, but the one I found most interesting was her views on parenting. Mrs. Kennedy was extremely private after the assassination of President Kennedy. Along with so many others, I was impressed that she managed to raise her children out of the public eye. They grew up to be intelligent, responsible, and successful adults. I don't remember many of the details about the interview, but one thing has stuck with me all of these years. I am paraphrasing here a bit, but the gist of what she said was this: "It doesn't matter how many great things you do, or how much you accomplish in this life, if your kids turn out bad, you have failed."

Wow! That is a powerful statement and oh so true. I was amazed that someone with so much prestige, who had great amounts of wealth, and was the recipient of so much adoration worldwide, would have gotten it right. You can be the best in your field professionally, have more money than your grandchildren's grandchildren could spend, but if your kids turn out rotten, YOU HAVE FAILED! The buck stops here. So many people make excuses about why their kids don't turn out to be responsible, contributing members of society. The laundry list is endless: it was the school's fault, their friends were a bad influence, it's the influence of television and music entertainers, the church failed to give them a moral foundation... The excuses go on and on, but the reality is this: the buck stops with the parents. It is our responsibility to raise children with good character.

Some role models in our society today leave a lot to be desired. One current example of this is the twenty-something year old daughter of a hotel tycoon, who recently published a book, giving young girls advice about handling issues they will face while growing up. This highly visible young woman is considered quite attractive, and she has been brought up with every luxury and every advantage that money can buy. Yet, she has had some serious decency issues brought forth in a very public way. Last year, a sex tape surfaced on the Internet. It was recorded when she was still a teenager, with a man almost ten years her senior. Though she claimed to be "embarrassed and humiliated" by the fact that this tape was made public, the more concerning fact was that the tape was made at all. Recently, Hustler magazine announced they were publishing earlier pictures of this same girl, again as a teenager, in a lesbian encounter at a nightclub. Wow! I read about things like this and I wonder, "Where were her parents?" Apparently money doesn't buy parenting skills, and having money doesn't give you good character.

The greatest task, the hardest challenge, the most profoundly rewarding experience we can have as parents, as responsible individuals, is to positively shape and develop the life of another human being. The success or

A View from the Parents' Corner

failure in this task lies, for the most part, squarely on the shoulders of the parents or adult charged with a child's upbringing. Of course, genetics play a role in how a child develops... some traits are present when kids "come out of the box". There are always going to be influences outside the home which will shape certain aspects of life. But the reality is that the buck always stops at home, in the hands of the adults.

People like to make excuses for their children's shortcomings (and their own) but they need to look no further than the mirror. Rarely have I seen a situation where the parents were doing everything "the right way" and the children still turned out bad. Of course, this is not absolute, however if the parents (or the adults) in the child's life are people of good character, committed to raising children with good character, the road will still be hard, but more often than not the results will prove rewarding in the end.

So what does it mean to raise children with good character and how do we go about it? According to the CHARACTER COUNTS!sm materials my children bring home from school, there are six core, universal values: trustworthiness, respect, responsibility, fairness, caring and citizenship. These are pillars of good character that are true across the board. Teach them. Enforce them. Advocate them. And definitely model them! Trustworthiness is a key ingredient in developing good character in our children. Trustworthiness encompasses honesty, integrity, loyalty, and promise-keeping, to name just a few. Young children, by nature, will fudge the truth, exaggerate frequently, and disown responsibility from "sticky situations".

I can remember an incident with my youngest sister when she was growing up that illustrates this point. When she was around the age of five, she retrieved a pair of scissors from the kitchen drawer and proceeded to sit on the floor and cut her own hair. Upon discovering Mary Katherine in the act, my mother asked her "Did you cut your hair?" "No" she answered. Bear in mind that she was sitting in the floor with the scissors at her feet and the hair scattered all over the floor. She knew she was in a lot of trouble; not only for cutting her hair, but for having my mother's scissors, which were off limits. Her first instinct was to lie. Needless to say, my mother dealt swiftly and clearly with both the haircutting and the lie. Mary Katherine never attempted to buzz her own hair again.

The point I was making in referring to this incident was that her first instinct was to lie in order to avoid trouble. This is an instinct we MUST cut off in our children, and we must do it early in their lives. They must learn that taking the punishment is preferable to telling the lie. This is a hard concept to teach unless as parents we practice what we preach. Gentle admonishments are usually enough in the young years to drive home the point that honesty is important. As children grow older, blatant dishonesty must be dealt with swiftly and firmly. I believe children are born with a sense of right and wrong and, if trained properly, do have a conscience that will bother them when they know they have done wrong. Dishonesty left unchecked for the duration of childhood leads to teenagers and later adults, with no problems lying and deceiving. In fact, some seem to have problems differentiating between truth and lies. If we drive home the point during childhood that there are not "degrees of truth" (i.e. there is no such thing as half-truths or white lies) then that line between what is right and wrong won't be so easily blurred.

Teaching loyalty and integrity to our children is equally important. Integrity, of course, involves standing up for what is right and what you believe in. It also involves the strength of character to not back down when what is "right" is not always what is popular. This is so hard to instill in our children, and is hard to "make it stick." This is particularly true in the teen years when peer pressure is so enormous. One way to help build this trait in our children is to role play with them. Give your child situations or scenarios in which they might find themselves having to take a stand. See what they say and how they think they would handle it. If they handle the mock situation in the appropriate manner, brag like crazy. If they handle the situation poorly or become stuck in not knowing how to handle it, this is where guidance and teaching by the parents come into play.

Loyalty can also be taught this way. Teaching our children not be "fair weather friends" is so important. As our kids get older and cliques become such an issue, our children must remain loyal to their true friends, even if their friends are not considered "cool" or "popular". I can remember an incident from my own childhood that when I think back on it, still makes me cringe. When I was in seventh grade, I rode the bus to school. I had a nice set of friends on the bus and never had any negative social issues myself. However, there was a girl named Hope who was always the last person picked up before we arrived at school. By the time the bus arrived for Hope, it was pretty full and everyone was paired off with their own friends. Hope was a shy, but sweet girl. For reasons I never knew, the other kids on the bus did not like her. In fact, they were down right mean to her. Because she was shy, she never popped it back to these bullies, which made the situation worse. No one would ever move over to let her sit down and there was always an embarrassing few minutes before she would finally find a seat somewhere toward the front. A rumor started circulating around the bus that Hope smelled bad and chants of "Hope needs soap" erupted. This went on for weeks and the driver did nothing to stop it. As I was always one of the first to be picked up in the morning and I always sat in the back, I had no interactions with Hope until one morning when I just couldn't stand the taunting anymore. Hope got on the bus this particular morning and took the empty seat right behind the driver. Immediately the chanting and taunting began. When the driver came to a stop light, I picked up my books and darted straight to the front of the bus and sat down next to Hope, who looked shocked.

"Hi." I said. "My name is Laura. Do you mind if I sit with you?" She looked confused for a moment, but then smiled. We chatted for the last few minutes of the ride before we arrived at school. She was a nice girl and guess what? She didn't smell odd at all. The pack mentality on that bus had made a poor girl's social life a living hell and no one would stand up for her, not even herself. When everyone got off the bus, a few people asked me why I had moved up to sit with Hope. My answer was simple... because she needed a friend. Hope and I remained friendly, though we were never close friends. But the fact that I was willing to take a stand on the bus that day put an end to a lot of the mistreatment that girl suffered at the hands of bullies on that bus.

A View from the Parents' Corner

I did not share this story in an effort to pat myself on the back, but rather to illustrate how one person can make a positive difference in someone else's life if they have the moral courage to make a stand. In a world where loyalty and integrity are in short supply, it is critical that we instill these traits in our children early.

The world teaches the ashen rule of "do unto others before they have a chance to do unto you." We, as responsible parents, must teach the "Golden Rule" and make respect a part of who our children ARE, not just what they should believe. People with good character show respect to everyone by being courteous, nonviolent, allowing others to maintain their dignity, behaving decently, and recognizing that others have a right to make choices.

"Pass the buck" parents have "pass the buck" children. Parents who refuse to accept responsibility for their actions teach this to their children through example. Have you ever forgotten to send in payment for your phone bill, then ranted and raved to the phone company when they shut off your phone? "I can't believe YOU shut off my phone. I only sent that payment in a few days late!" That's only a stone's throw away from a child who blames the teacher when he doesn't turn in his assignment because "he didn't understand what the teacher wanted him to do." Taking ownership of mistakes is being responsible. Living up to one's obligations is being responsible. This is something that must be taught to our children: it isn't innate. We are not living up to OUR responsibilities as parents if we don't teach doing your part, pursuing excellence, fixing mistakes, and self-control to our children.

Teaching discipline and implementing discipline is crucial

in the home. Children can not grow up to be successful, happy adults without learning discipline. Let me repeat that again... children can not grow up to be successful, happy adults without learning discipline. Being disciplined involves many things... patience, endurance, persistence, but most of all, self-control. Children crave discipline. When a parent uses discipline effectively in the home, a child sees the importance of discipline, and embraces those concepts internally. Parents often shirk the responsibility of disciplining their children for the simple reason that it is time-consuming and unpleasant. We must have a system in place within our homes where there are defined consequences for inappropriate behavior. And here's the hard part... we must be consistent in enforcing those consequences. When parents are not committed to following through with consequences, any attempts at disciplining the child will be largely ineffective. For example, in our home, we enforce the "three bite rule" at dinner. If one of our children does not want to finish his dinner, he does not get ice cream or some other treat that the other children will be receiving. If he refuses his three bites, it's no T.V. for the rest of the night or next day, depending on the time of day. This is not a popular rule in our home, but we have enforced it religiously, and therefore, the kids know EXACTLY what the consequences are for not doing what is expected.

Our children know that David and I are disciplinarians, but I also go to great lengths to explain why we have the rules we have and why the consequences are what they are. They know that our discipline is out of a place of love. Even when disciplining in our home for a serious offense, and I have to pop open my "big can of whoop" (which doesn't happen often) my children know that I still love

A View from the Parents' Corner

them dearly and their displeasure with me soon subsides. Our children respect David and me as the authorities in the home. They don't challenge our right to discipline them. Our children show self-control and I believe this has a lot to do with the principles of self-discipline we have worked hard to instill.

The good thing about consistency in discipline is that if you hold the line with your children, following through with consequences EVERY time, this is not something you will find yourself having to do very often. Children who have learned what it means to live with the consequences of poor choices, will soon learn to make better ones.

Our children need to see us being disciplined adults. Self-control is such an important thing to teach early. Juvenile detention centers and jails are full of people who have never learned discipline and self control. This is so important for our children's social and emotional development. As I said, children long for discipline. They want their parents to show they care for them by teaching them discipline and enforcing it. We do our children a great disservice when we fail to do this well. There is no one set of techniques for discipline that works in every home, for every child. As parents, we must find which approach is most effective for our own child. When we have honed in on the one that works... consistency, consistency, consistency. It is the only way to effectively discipline, and to teach discipline.

Our children need to grow up learning what it means to "play fair" in a world that teaches them that it is "every man for himself." Play games together as a family. Highlight the importance of playing by the rules. Divide household and yard tasks. Talk about fairness when dividing things among family members. Remember that equal is not always fair.

Our children need to grow up knowing that it is important to be caring individuals. In the "me universe", children must show a caring side; they must show empathy for others. As parents we must teach this by example. Have you ever seen an able-bodied homeless person panning for money at a red light and made a snide remark about them in front of your children? Ever said "go get a job, pal!" in your mind, or maybe even out loud in your car? Wouldn't it be better to crack your window and slide out a dollar to teach your child a lesson about caring and compassion, instead of a lesson about avoidance or maybe contempt? Isn't that what good citizenship is all about? Good citizenship is about doing your part to make our world the best it can be. There are endless numbers of service projects you can do with your children to show that good citizenship is active citizenship. Good citizens in society... isn't that what we want our children to be? The buck stops here, guys. It always does.

Raising children with good character is a daunting task. It seems like the world stacks up obstacles against our efforts and makes it an almost impossible task. It is possible. We cannot falter in our efforts. The responsibility is enormous. This is why it is so sad that people can become parents in a biological sense even when they are unwilling or unable to accept the great challenges and responsibilities that go along with it. The rewards are great, but so is the sacrifice. There is no room for selfishness in parenting. The child's well-being always comes first... end of story. If this is not the case, the parenting experience will be fraught with problems. I have never chosen to look at it as a "sacrifice", but as a privilege and every good parent I have ever known has viewed it this way.

In parenting children of good character, we are not going to "get it right" every time. We are human, we all make mistakes. Our job is to admit mistakes, struggle openly, and commit to doing better. While there is some room for error, there's no room for failure... and the buck stops here.

16. Television/Movie No-No's

I recently saw a commercial on Nickelodeon "promoting" eating healthy foods. In this commercial, it pointed out that some healthy foods, such as beans and certain vegetables, cause gas. The last line of the commercial stated "be smart, know your farts, and let them rip!" Upon hearing this crude humor, I thought to myself, "Is it really necessary to use that kind of humor to make a point, particularly when it is targeted at kids?" Anything for a laugh, is it?

If the love of money is the root of all evil, then I would like to put forth the premise that the love of television is a heaping load of fertilizer that helps most any evil tree grow out of control. Television may be the worst invention of the twentieth century. In my opinion, it's the worst thing that ever happened to the homelife in this country. I know this is a strong statement to make. I also know this is not a popular view, particularly in a world that enjoys the benefit of having several hundred channels within the click of a remote control.

I grew up watching Sesame Street and Mister Rogers as a child. Later, I graduated to Happy Days as an older child, before eventually moving on to General Hospital in high school and college. I was hooked on television, just like every other couch potato kid, who preferred to be entertained while sitting on my derriere, rather than doing something creative (or at least productive). My mother was a soap addict, and still is. I remember passing through the family room shortly after lunch and always catching a little glimpse of "love in the afternoon." Of course, my mother would warn me, "don't look!" but I would always take a little peek anyway.

When television was first becoming popular during the 1950's and early 1960's, the programming that was provided was entertaining and wholesome. I still like watching reruns of "I love Lucy." In my opinion, that is the funniest show to ever run on television. I think I have seen each and every episode at least a dozen times; I can recall the dialog word for word and I still laugh at every punchline. It didn't use crude humor, off-colored jokes or innuendo to provoke a laugh. The only show I can think of in recent memory to hold itself to such a high standard was "The Cosby Show" back in the mid 1980's. Since then, the programming the networks have been marketing as "family television" has been a steady stream of mindless junk.

I have to relate a recent incident in our home one afternoon after school. I was in the kitchen preparing dinner while our older three children were in the family room watching a "family" show on a "family" channel. I was only hearing bits and pieces of the conversation going on between the children, but one phrase was uttered that spun me around on my heels and stopped me cold in my tracks. I don't know what was said previously, but I clearly heard Laurie say "No, Chad... I don't want to." Chad and Joey both giggled and said "No really means yes... girls always mean the opposite of what they say, so no really means yes!" Then they proceeded to chase her around the room.

WHOA! TIME OUT! "BOYS! COME HERE NOW!" I shouted from the kitchen. "WHAT DID YOU SAY? REPEAT THAT FOR ME ONE MORE TIME!" I demanded.

A View from the Parents' Corner

Chad's eyes got as big as saucers. "Girls mean the opposite of what they say?" he offered slowly, not knowing that what he had said was all kinds of wrong. "Who told you that?" I asked him. "Where did you hear that?" He told me he had heard it on one of the "family" shows that he was allowed to watch in the afternoon. This burned me up, big time! I was not mad at my son. He was just repeating what he had heard. I was furious that something like this was said on a show that targets children and disguises itself as a safe family show. I explained to both boys that this was completely wrong. I pointed out that I am a girl too, (though they don't really think of me in those terms) and I asked them if they have EVER known me to mean the opposite of what I say about ANYTHING. Of course, they dropped their heads and said no. What Chad said, of course, was said in complete innocence. But there is great danger in letting a statement like that go unchallenged. An attitude like that with a ten year old boy may result in something relatively harmless, like his sister getting tickled unmercifully. An attitude like that left unchallenged in the mind of a sixteen or seventeen year old male might lead to a girl in trouble in the backseat of his car.

It's so challenging in today's world to raise children with good character. There is so much to overcome in the negative images that bombard our children daily. You only have to look just beyond public television to find it. During our children's early years, there is plenty of wholesome, worthwhile programming to watch... Sesame Street, Barney, Arthur, just to name a few. But once the kids are school aged, television viewing becomes tricky. There are plenty of educational programs on the science/health channels. But these are not the shows the kids generally want to watch. They want to head straight for cartoon channels. This is a huge pet peeve of mine.

Have you ever really watched the cartoons targeted at our children today? When I was growing up, I was a huge fan of Scooby Doo and Bugs Bunny. Today's cartoons are a totally different breed. My kids' favorite cartoon has been one I'll characterize as "an anal retentive pants-wearing sponge." (Yes, I'm opinionated.) I can't see what is the least bit appealing about this show. I have never really seen anything "wrong" with this show other than it is a mindless, complete waste of time (and in my opinion, not the least bit entertaining, but then, I'm not a four-year old!).

In the last few years, cartoons like Pokemon and Yu-Gi-Oh have become extremely popular. I've been very concerned with the messages that these shows send. These shows do not promote the essential elements of good character. I have found that these shows, and others like it, often portray the characters being smart- mouthed, sarcastic, disrespectful, confrontational, and at times, unfair. And this is family television? Children's programming? Is this what we really want our children to be viewing? Folks, this is scary. Are the lessons they internalize from these shows really going to promote good healthy attitudes? I don't think so. I think it just de-sensitizes our children towards bad behavior. How are children going to develop the qualities of good character — trustworthiness, respect, responsibility, fairness, caring, and good citizenship — if they are constantly being taught the opposite in the "entertainment" they are viewing? David and I recently made a decision that is going to make us extremely unpopular in our own home; we are getting rid of cable television. By the time you read this, cable television in our home will be long gone! There was a collective cry throughout our home when we made the announcement; wailing and gnashing of teeth. But we are sticking to our guns on this one. We refuse to continue to pay hundreds of dollars per year to have our children's minds filled with junk and their character corrupted. Okay... that may be a little melodramatic, but you get the point. I am sure they will go through a period of withdrawal (please mom! Just one show... I can't live with out it!) But in time, they will adjust and find something else to do with their time other than having their brains turn to mush.

Movies are another area of concern. As my oldest son is approaching the "tween" years, (too old for Disney-type movies, too young for teenage movies, which I define as PG-13) it is hard to know what is appropriate for him. We recently watched Disney's Pirates of the Caribbean which is PG-13; we thought it was a little intense in places, but basically okay. I am sure most PG-13 movies would not get our stamp of approval at this point because of language content. De-sensitizing our children to such things is not healthy. I know we can't put off their exposure to it forever, but we can for now.

The first really intense movie I ever saw was "Fatal Attraction" in 1986. I was sixteen years old and this was the first R-rated movie I had ever seen. I went with my best friend from school and we were quite proud to have bought a ticket without being asked for proof of age. I was a pretty naive sixteen year old and the language in that movie was the worst I had ever heard. In all honesty, I remember it did bother me to hear the "f-word' used over and over again. I was raised knowing that this is not an acceptable way to talk and it felt a little trashy to hear it used so casually. In regards to the heavy sex scenes in that movie, you could have heard a pin drop in that movie theater when Michael Douglas and Glenn Close were making it in the kitchen sink. I had never seen a simulated sex scene that was so graphic. I think I might have breathed twice, and swallowed hard once. I remember leaning over to my friend and asking "Do you think people ever really do it in the sink?" I received an education that day, one that my mother would have lived in church for if she had known. Those things bothered me on that day, on the first exposure. It didn't take too many more exposures for me to not be bothered at all. Desensitization is a dangerous thing for our kids, especially when it happens at a young age.

I am often floored when I see parents buying tickets to movies that are rated R and are taking young children inside with them. Do they really expect their children not to pick up on some of the filthiness that they see or hear? When messages about life are sent to our children over and over again, even when they are messages that are not true, it can be hard for us as parents to overcome.

I hate seeing television shows that portray children mouthing off to adults or portray the adults as "the stupid ones" and the kids as "the clever ones". If I see one more show on television in which a kid is answering his parents in a smart-mouth, sarcastic tone of voice, and the parents just stand there like stupid-doofs without reprimanding the bad behavior, I might just have to shoot a hole through my television. I could go on and on, but I will stop here. In a world where parents are content to allow the television to babysit their children, and allow the television to shape their view of the world, it's no wonder we have schools and juvenile detention centers full of children who don't respect adults, authority, other children, or themselves. Good character doesn't happen by accident. It happens by conscientious parents taking the reigns in their children's lives and assuming responsibility of teaching them what it means to be a productive member of society — what it means to have good character. Children can't learn these important lessons on television, because, for the most part, they just aren't there. When televisions are commonplace in kitchens, it often replaces conversations around the dinner table. When televisions are placed in our children's bedrooms and hold them captive for hours at a time, this is dangerous because they dis-engage in family time. Our society's children have become a group of overweight, underactive couch potatoes who are strongly influenced by what they watch. Family life has been traded away in many homes for the small price of a monthly cable television subscription. That is really pretty sad, if you think about it. Sad, but often, unfortunately, very true.

17. Toys, Toys, Everywhere!

In this high tech world that we live in, it has become increasingly difficult to entertain our children with simple toys. Back in "the good ol' days" a pile of blocks and our imaginations were enough to keep us entertained for hours. I can remember playing outside all summer long with nothing more than a kick ball or my bicycle. But today's kids are bombarded with electronic gizmos and high tech toys that make a simple kick ball seem like a truly dull toy.

When Chad was in kindergarten, my parents came to town for a visit. Upon leaving, they wanted to buy the kids a small toy as a goodbye present. When my mother asked Chad what he wanted, he said "I would like a 'good toy'." Needing clarification on that answer, my mother asked him what a good toy was. "Oh Mimi!" he said. "A good toy is one that flashes lights and makes a lot of noise!" Oh my, how times have changed! The more bells and whistles a toy has, the better.

In thinking about the never ending quest for "bigger, better toys", I am frequently surprised at the new toys offered up by today's toy manufacturers. As the holidays were approaching this year, I asked my older three children to start complying their Christmas "wish list". Actually, I shop for Christmas all year long and am usually finished with ninety-nine percent of it by September. However, I always encourage then to put together a list so I can see how well I did in shopping ahead for each of them.

This year brought a whole new list of surprises for me and sent me scrambling for alternatives to their suggestions. Top number one wish list item for both Chad and Joey: Stinkblasters. When I read this I thought to myself "WHAT is a stinkblaster?" Then I asked myself "Do I really want to know what it is?" The boys informed me that this was THE hot item this year; a real must have toy. I didn't know what it was, but it didn't sound too appealing to me, either.

Later that day, almost as if a toy company executive was working on behalf of my boys, a commercial for this little gem of a toy ran during one of their kid shows. And there it was... THE STINKBLASTER. A gun-type toy, that when "shot" makes a noise and then emits a foul smell; thus, the Stinkblaster. I'm sitting there watching this commercial and thinking "A gun that expels gas? Is that really healthy?" As if raising respectful, polite children with good manners is not hard enough without a toy manufacturer making a bizarre, smelly toy that encourages rude behavior.

Who would have ever thought to invent such a toy? I can almost picture the creative team and toy executives sitting around a large table, in a corporate office somewhere, pitching around ideas for new toys for this production year. I bet some little peon, who probably cheated in his creative writing classes, and probably spent much of his early years in school "pulling fingers" and unloading spitballs, piped up after having his fifth latte of the morning and said "I know what we should do... let's create a f_ _ting gun and market it to every pre-pubescent boy in the universe, who still thinks that expelling gas is funny!" There was probably a collective roar of approval from every male executive in the room, to whom the concept still appealed to his inner child, that drowned out the groans of disapproval from the level-headed women in the group. Do men ever get over thinking that gas is funny? I wonder if there has ever been a scientific study exploring this issue.

Anyway, so what do you name a gun with a flatulence problem, so as to market it in a way that will not turn off every mother with cash? "Call it a Stinkblaster!" someone probably suggested. "To make it sound like a weapon of some kind... a weapon that fights evildoers by paralyzing them with a deadly smell... a weapon that promotes the triumph of good over evil with the mere expulsion of smelly air... that's how we'll promote it!" If only all the evil in the world could be eradicated with a puff of bad wind, what a wonderful world this would be! This is the type of toy I would have expected to see in the "crude humor" section at Spencer's. Apparently, this toy has enough appeal to make it's way to the mainstreams of Toys-R-Us and Wal-mart. Whatever happened to a good ol' whoopie cushion? When I was a kid, that was always good for a cheap laugh. Do kids really need to point a play "weapon" at their friends and take them out with one foul blast? A tooting toy? What's our world coming to, anyway? Maybe it's just the woman in me, but foul air is not funny, in any way, shape or form. Needless to say, the Stinkblaster will not find its way under the Christmas tree in our house this year.

The boys aren't the only ones with "the toys from way out there..." High on the list of five year old Laurie is a toy called a "Bratz" doll. I probably don't have to explain where my problem lies with this one. Forget cute little princesses with crowns or even Barbie in her swimsuit. These little Bratz dolls take the cake. I can picture a board room full of female toy executives, downing their power coffee and popping their anti-PMS pills, trying to decide how to push off these little dolls, who have obviously gone through puberty, onto unsuspecting little girls who are just dying to act "all grown up". A "Bratz" doll... are you kidding me? Why not call it the "Cindy Imahoe" doll or maybe the "Donna Wannadoome" doll? I wish you could see the sarcasm dripping from my fingertips as I type.

Why can't little girls just be little girls for awhile? Why do young girls need a teenage-looking doll to play with? Doesn't that influence come along soon enough without the help of toy manufacturers? I don't see why this world needs a bratty doll. Don't we have enough bratty children in the world without validating bratty behavior with it's own line of dolls? Okay, I'm off on a tangent, I know that. Maybe the "Bratz" dolls really aren't any worse than Barbie dolls (not that I'm crazy about her either) but just the name "Bratz" is irritating. To me, a "brat" is a very unappealing person. I don't know why toy executives would market a toy to young girls that in an unconscious way says that being a brat is acceptable, or worse, desirable. Maybe that is not the intent, but it sure seems that way to me. There will be no Bratz in our house; that's for sure. Laurie will have to make do with a Tinkerbell doll instead... a few more years for her in Neverland are just fine with me.

The high tech world is just amazing, isn't it? Our boys don't even have to go outside to play baseball; they can just play a virtual game of it on the television. Forget playing a game of "tag, you're it", this generation plays

A View from the Parents' Corner

tag with paint guns. This generation is definitely the generation of "the bigger, the better". Our Children no longer need to use their imaginations because machines and gadgets do all the work for them. Toy manufacturers do not do much to help promote creativity in children. They may argue that today's video games promote good hand/eye coordination (if so, my two year old son and his Gameboy will be ready to take the state driving exam next week), but this still doesn't excuse the poor quality of many of the toys marketed to children these days. My boys like to "duel" with Yu-Gi-Oh cards... what's fun about that? I can't figure that one out, but it sure is popular right now. What ever happened to trading baseball cards and pitching footballs in the yard? Whatever happened to tea parties and easy-bake ovens?

Of course, a really principled parent might say "I will not fall into that technological trap! I didn't have all those gizmos and gadgets and it didn't hurt me! I will not buy all of that junk!" But the reality of the world we live in is that kids want to play with what they and their friends perceive as "cool toys" and they want to play at the houses of the kids with the "cool toys". Since I want my children and their friends to WANT to hang out at OUR house rather than somewhere else, I do go along with "the program" a lot of the time, I'm ashamed to admit. I wish the toy manufacturers did more to make our jobs as parents easier, or at least not market toys like Stinkblasters and Bratz dolls on commercials aimed at younger children. (if those items must be made at all). Technological progress isn't always a good thing. Sometimes the simple things are still the best things. Anyone for a game of dress-up or "two hand touch" in the yard?

"Choosing the right partner for the Parent's Corner is so important to it being a joyous experience. I know in my heart that I chose the right partner."

Pastel Colors

18. The Story Of Us

Long before there were midnight feedings, diapers, little league games and ballet recitals, there was us. In everyone's lives there are certain crossroads, at which the decisions you make there will alter the course of your life. Meeting David set my life on a course which I could have never foreseen, and has taken us on a journey of great personal joy. I don't believe in accidents in this life, and I believe the events which brought our lives together were by design.

Our journey toward the Parents' Corner began as a "blink, and you could have missed it" encounter in September 1988. I was a college freshmen, mulling over an invitation to pledge a sorority at the university I was attending, but far more excited about being a Kappa Sigma "little sister" and all that went along with that. I loved the new-found independence that goes along with being in college, and I didn't want to be tied down to anything or anyone. For six months, I had been dating a steady boyfriend from high school when I suddenly had the urge to "be free" and decided to break the news to him one night early in my freshman year of college. On this particular night, I had plans to attend a Kappa Sigma frat party, which I had been looking forward to for several days. I had the invitation taped to the mirror in my bedroom, and had every intention of going. But, on the night of the party, I met my boyfriend for dinner and dropped the bomb that I wanted "to see other people", but was still open to dating him, too. This did not go over well, and I felt guilty for hurting him. He asked me to go with him that night to a going away party for a friend of his. Out of a sense of obligation, I reluctantly agreed to go and skipped the frat party. This decision to attend the party with him, and not the frat party, would be the decision that would change my life forever.

This going away party was relatively small (thirty people, maybe), and I only knew one other person at the party besides my now ex-boyfriend. It happened to be a guy I had worked with at a grocery store during the summer before my senior year of high school. We had been friends, but I had not seen him in at least a year. It was good to see him, but I was far more interested in the friend he had with him... a tall, good looking guy with beautiful blue eyes. He was wearing a red muscle shirt, and a tight pair of Guess jeans. I had noticed him immediately upon walking into the party, but I had no intentions of acting on my interest.

My ex-boyfriend was drinking at this party, and I was not. Soon I became bored with the whole scene and asked him to take me home. He wanted to stay, so I waited, and waited... and waited some more. A couple of "confidence building" drinks in, and my ex-boyfriend came up to me in front of a group of people and planted a full-mouth kiss on me, which was most unwelcome due to the fact that I had just broken up with him. Needless to say, I leveled him in front of his friends, which prompted him to call me a "not so nice name" in front of these people. He crawled into another room. I sat down by myself in the den. Soon after, the tall, good-looking guy I had noticed when I came in, was standing over me, delivering the best pick-up line I had ever heard. He opened with "Is that guy being a jerk to you? If you were with me, I wouldn't treat you like that!" I was a little stunned, but mostly impressed, and

A View from the Parents' Corner

invited him to sit down. While my ex-boyfriend spent the rest of the evening getting plastered with his friends, David and I spent the rest of the evening talking. I kept thinking, "Look at those beautiful blue eyes." I thought he looked like a young Paul Newman (still do). There was something about this guy that just struck me as different from anyone else I had dated; he seemed like an old soul. We had so much in common... and boy, did we have chemistry... lots of chemistry. I was hoping that he was as interested in me as I was in him. I think I played it pretty cool, at least I was trying to. I don't remember giggling like a silly school girl with a major crush, but I was really digging him. I didn't exactly picture him being the father of my children at that point, but I would have been very disappointed to leave that party without plans to see him again.

As I was getting ready to leave, (by this point I had managed to retrieve the keys from my now impaired ex-boyfriend) we traded phone numbers. David called me three days later, and we went out the very next weekend. After our first date, David broke it off with the girl he had been dating for eight months, and I told my ex-boyfriend to take a permanent hike, and the rest is, as they say, history. At eighteen, my desire for "freedom" had me believing I might never get married. Meeting David changed everything for me. Three and a half years, and a book's worth of stories later, we got married, and soon we were partners in the Parents' Corner.

I have wondered if I should have sent a thank you note to my ex-boyfriend for putting me together with David. If he had not insisted on going to that party, I would not have met my husband. If I had gone to that fraternity party that night, my life would be completely different. I still have the invitation to that fraternity party in my college scrapbook. I consider it "the road not taken", a reminder of how close my life came to taking a different turn. I am profoundly grateful that I missed that fraternity party. The boy I fell in love with in college, grew into the man with whom I share my life and greatest joy—our children. Choosing the right partner for the Parents' Corner is so important to it being a joyous experience. I know in my heart that I chose the right partner. The story of "us" became the story of my life; one that I am happy to share with you.

Our wedding day, 1992

19. Fighting Infertility: The Birth Of Chad

First let me start off by saying with pride that I am the mother of five wonderful children. And yes, we planned it that way. It is amazing how people look at you when they count five little heads running around a shopping cart. "You sure are brave to take five children with you to the grocery store!" I have heard this a few times. I think to myself, "How many am I suppose to take with me? We all have to eat!"

People make comments along the lines of "Oh my! Five kids... you must have your hands full!" (even though they are behaving perfectly and not disturbing anyone) The implication being that the fact that I have five must be an almost unbearable load. Of course, I know what they are really thinking... "She must be crazy" or "That poor little ignorant Georgia girl with that thick hillbilly accent! Doesn't she know what caused all those babies to get here? Doesn't she know to quit hiding out in that haystack behind the barn, with that redneck husband of hers?" Sometimes I want to say to those nosy folks that "Yes, I have five children!" and then bombard them with tidbits of information like, "Guess what? I have a college education and the accent is just one I developed to highlight my southern charm! "(and by the way, my redneck husband is actually a college educated man from Michigan).

Usually, the first thing people ask me when they find out that we have five children under the age of ten is if we are Catholics or maybe Mormons. I kid you not. Mostly, I think this is just incredibly rude. My stock answer to this question is "No, we are just overachieving Protestants who wanted a bunch of kids!" Another favorite question to answer: "Are they all yours?" No, I take the neighbors kids to the grocery store just for fun! And my hands down favorite; "You have five kids? Do you plan to have any more?" I usually resist my kneejerk response, which would be to say out loud, "That's really none of your business," in favor of something along the lines of "Not more than two or three more!" It is amazing how being out in public with a large family gives complete strangers a feeling of entitlement to ask personal, and at times rude, questions.

Truthfully, I don't remember if David and I ever said an actual number of kids we planned to have when we first married, but we knew we wanted a large family if it was possible. During my early twenties, it looked as if we might not be able to have children of our own. But, ten years and five kids later, I am happy to report that we are firmly planted in the Parents' Corner with a wealth of experience and wonderful memories to share.

My first glimpse from the Parents' Corner began in October of 1993. I was twenty-three years old and had just abandoned a three year stint in radio and was a graduate student at Georgia State University, studying to become a therapist. On a cold Monday morning in Atlanta, I sat anxiously in the lab area of my GYN's office while I waited for the results of my pregnancy test. I was a few days late, but I had been late before. I tapped my foot nervously, and I felt a little nauseated. A somewhat ambiguous home pregnancy test I had taken over the weekend left me with butterflies in my stomach. So was I, or wasn't I? I tried not to get my hopes up, but I could not help it. I was staring down at the floor, waiting for the long minutes to pass, when I saw a pair of shoes step in front of me and I looked

A View from the Parents' Corner

up. Brenda, a very sweet nurse in my GYN's office, had a big grin on her face and she said sweetly "Congratulations, Laura, it's positive!" It was very early—not "the morning after", but pretty close to it. Nonetheless, I was definitely pregnant. The confirmation of what I already suspected, hit me like a bolt of lightning. I felt my heart race, and I am sure the grin on my face lit up the room. Every one of the nurses who worked in the office came up and gave me a hug. Every one who worked there knew what a triumph this was for us. They knew we had overcome great odds to get to this point. These ladies and my doctor had been a great source of encouragement for us in all our efforts to start a family and they were genuinely happy that we were finally pregnant.

I asked to use the phone to call David with the good news. We were both so stunned—not because we didn't want to be pregnant, we very much did. But we had been trying for almost a year without success. As a matter of fact, I had an appointment with a fertility clinic at Emory University the following month. I must have sounded downright giddy when I called the clinic to cancel my appointment. "I won't be needing it!" I declared to the unsuspecting voice on the phone, "We are pregnant!"

You see, the odds of us being able to have a biological child were not great. When I was nineteen, I had a benign ovarian tumor the size of a small grapefruit removed, along with my right ovary and right fallopian tube. I had a severe case of endometriosis that had done a lot of damage to my reproductive system and often women with endometriosis have trouble getting pregnant. I remember being absolutely crushed when I got my diagnosis. The thought of not being able to have children was almost unbearable. David, who was my fiance' at the time, assured me that we would have children someday, one way or another. I was not so convinced. Fortunately, I had a wonderful GYN, Dr. Mark Davis, who oversaw my care and made sure that what I did have left in terms of my reproductive ability stayed healthy, while I finished my undergraduate work and, really, while I finished growing up. I can say without a doubt that were it not for Dr. Davis's care on my behalf, I would not be writing this book today. Why? The simple reason is this: I think it is likely that we would not have been able to have biological children. Now five kids and all these years later, I can look back at that stressful and uncertain time in our lives and smile. For a couple that was not suppose to have an easy time having children, I'd say we've done alright! I will always be grateful to Dr. Davis for his role in our lives.

I had my first ultrasound at six weeks. I remember putting on my glasses to be able to see every detail that the screen would reveal. All I could see was a little bean shape and a little blip flashing. "What is that?" I asked the technician performing the scan. "Oh! wait a minute" she said, as she turned up the volume knob on the machine. "That's your baby's heart beating!" David and I just stared at the screen in complete amazement. Hearing that little heart beating made it all so real... I was carrying life inside me and the proof was right there. "Looks like a kidney bean to me!" my husband said, while grinning ear to ear. I just could not take my eyes off the screen. "I am really going to be a mother!" I thought to myself and an enormous sense of responsibility flowed through me. For the first time in my life, I felt there was something bigger and more important than myself. For the first time in my life, I felt like an adult.

A View from the Parents' Corner

There was a song that came out a few years ago by a popular band named Creed. The name of the song is "With Arms Wide Open." For those of you who may not be familiar with it, the lyrics describes the emotions that the writer of this song felt the first time he found out he was going to be a father. When I heard this song for the first time, it brought back in my mind the feelings I had when I found out that I was going to be a mother... the tremendous joy, the weight of the responsibility, the desire to show my child every wonderful thing that life has to offer, the desire to be a better person — to be worthy of this amazing gift that has been given to me. I was on cloud nine and I never really came down from it.

When I was about ten weeks pregnant, I dreamed I was having a little boy. At nineteen weeks, an ultrasound confirmed that indeed he was a boy. I almost fell off of the table. You see, I came from a family of all girls. As a matter of fact, even my extended family, my cousins, are mostly females. It had not really occurred to me (at least during waking hours) that I might be having a boy... we just didn't make those in our family! I had the tech check between the legs one more time just to be sure that the umbilical cord was not being mistaken for the "family jewels". But our son was not shy and he gave us a good peak to confirm that, indeed, I was carrying a son!

The pregnancy went by slowly, as we prepared for the baby's arrival. By week twenty, I was feeling him kicking frequently. Even after five pregnancies, I still think this is an absolutely amazing feeling. I remember telling a lady at church who was asking how my pregnancy was progressing, what a miracle it was to feel life moving around inside you. She said something that really stuck with me, "You know Laura, pregnancy is the only time in life that God needs your help in making a miracle happen." I found that to be profound and true. I have never forgotten that conversation. I am not sure how anyone could say that an unborn baby does not represent life. I am not sure how anyone who has ever carried a child within her body could be pro-choice.

On the lighter side, toward the end of the pregnancy, the last big hurdle we had to overcome was a name. We could not settle on a name, as I wanted it to be "perfect". Initially, we chose "Brandon". That's what we called him up until the seventh month. However, a chance encounter with an icky little kid named Brandon sent me scrambling for a new name. I remember racing home, calling my husband at work, and declaring that we MUST come up with a new name. I just could not call my sweet precious baby "Brandon". It conjured up images in my mind of this other obnoxious kid. Finally we decided on Charles David, after my father and my husband. I thought that "Chad" was a sweet combination of the two names and that's what we call him.

At 37 1/2 weeks, our baby made a hasty entrance into the world.. When I arrived at the hospital, I was already dilated to 9 cm. There was no time for an epidural and I was freaking out. "I want drugs!" I shouted and then begged. The nurse who was prepping me for delivery asked if I had taken any breathing classes or been through the Lamaze program. "No!" I answered. I had not planned to have a natural delivery. Pain medicine fed straight through a drug line seemed pretty natural to me! She gave me a quick lesson in breathing through my contractions, but the contractions were coming so hard

A View from the Parents' Corner

and so quickly, I could hardly catch my breath. I was out of my head in pain and scared to death of having this baby without pain medication. "What do I need to do?" I asked the doctor who was on call. Then this doctor, a male doctor no less, said one of the stupidest things anyone has ever said in the history of the world... "The best way to stop the pain is just to have the baby!" I was looking for pain relief, not a smart-aleck answer. (note: I know that Dr. Davis, or any female doctor who had experienced the pain of labor, would never have said something so stupid). If I had not needed this man to catch my baby, who was about to fall out between my legs, I swear I would have shoved the heel of my right foot, conveniently positioned near his head in a stirrup, right up his nose. "You are going to have to focus and push, Mrs. Hull" he said. The fact that he was calling me "Mrs. Hull" was irritating me, too. Call me crazy, but when someone is shining a hot light between my legs and has his head parked between my knees, I want him to call me by my first name.

"Push, Mrs. Hull, he's right here," the doctor said. I remember gripping the rails on the bed and just bearing down with all of the strength I had in me. I was ready for this labor (and the pain) to be over. About five minutes and three hard pushes later, our beautiful son was born — a little less than thirty minutes after we arrived at the hospital. I listened for him to take his first breath, and that's when I took mine. I left an old life behind that day and have never looked back. Suddenly, nothing I had ever done before seemed to have any importance to me like what I was getting ready to do. From the time the nurse placed him in my arms, I found a new and great purpose in my life. I am a mother. I am HIS mother. What in the world had I ever done to deserve such an honor? That is truly how I felt, and still feel. I have felt that way with the birth of each of my five children.

There is something truly special about watching your husband hold your child for the first time. I will never forget the look on David's face the first time he held our son. The sweetness and tenderness with which he held and talked to Chad was one of the most touching things I have ever witnessed. I knew I loved him before, but seeing this took the love I felt for him to a new level. I had my first look at my husband in his role as a father and it was amazing to behold. He has been this way with all of our children. We both feel like our lives have been blessed a thousand times over; each of our children is such a wonderful gift. The wonder and miracle of bringing a child into this world is not something that diminishes with future children. It's no less special with child two or ten. People have actually said that we must be crazy for having five children. They just can't comprehend how it is possible to manage the workload involved in raising them all. I just smile because even though they cannot see how rewarding and fulfilling it is, I know that the human heart has an amazing capacity for love. There's more than enough room for each and every child that blesses our lives.

I know beyond a shadow of a doubt that I became a better person when I became a mother. For the first time in my life, I knew what it meant to love someone unselfishly and unconditionally... the purest form of love that exists. Raising a large family is definitely a lot of work. Sometimes our home is a little chaotic, and it's almost always loud. But it is busting at the seams with love, joy and dreams for the endless possibilities that each one of

A View from the Parents' Corner

these young lives possesses and the hope for a lifetime of happiness that lies ahead.

Our first family photo, minutes after Chad's birth

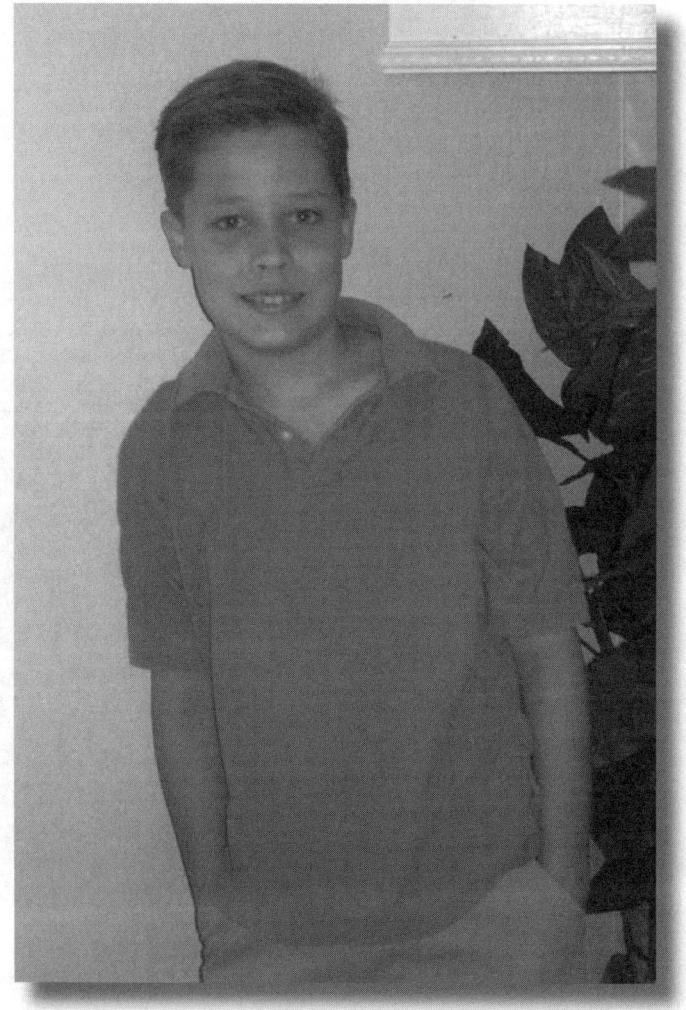

Our Chad

20. The Woes Of The First Born

For a long time, I have felt sorry for young Prince William of Great Britain. The responsibility that young man must shoulder and the expectations heaped upon him are unrealistic. From the time he was born, the world has watched and wondered what would become of this future king. Of course, William never asked for any of this, he just made the mistake of being born first. Actually, I would imagine that saying "he made the mistake" would not be accurate, because to say that implies that he had a choice in the matter. He had the misfortune of being born first. That may sound harsh, given that he was born to a life of such privilege. But his life is not his own and that is because so much is expected of him. Just think of his brother, Harry. He has all the same wealth and privilege, but a lot less is expected of him. You may be wondering why I chose to mention these brothers. It is simple. These same rules of responsibility and expectations for the first born are true, albeit on a smaller scale, in most families. You don't have to be first in line to a throne to have high expectations heaped on top of you. It happens every day, in many homes, everywhere.

The role of the oldest child is not an easy gig. Just as parents often slip into their perceived roles with thoughtless ease, this tends to be true amongst the children as well. I remember studying in college about the characteristics of the oldest child. I have special sympathy for my oldest son, Chad. I, too, grew up the oldest child in my family, and I, more or less, thought my lot in life stunk. Parents are much harder on the oldest child. It was true when I was growing up and it is still true today in my own home. I truly believe this stems from the intense efforts we direct toward everything that pertains to the well-being of the child, particularly the first child. I remember being such an intense young mother with my oldest son, Chad. I was a schedule hound and a germ freak! I carried a can of Lysol with me everywhere and no one was exempted from my sterilization efforts! I had him counting baby food jars at twelve months of age and he was potty trained before his second birthday. I knew "Good Night Moon" word for word, and I hummed Mozart in my sleep. I snapped to attention every time he whimpered and our son never had a case of diaper rash, because a diaper never stayed on long enough to be a problem. NEVER! Okay, I was really intense. I certainly learned, as I got older, wiser, and distracted by a houseful of kids, that this kind of intensity is not necessary all the time, but that approach of parenting to our oldest son has been something I have had to make a conscious effort to fight. Sometimes I am successful, and sometimes I am not.

At the beginning of the school year in fourth grade, Chad was selected to be his classroom representative on student council. I have to tell you, I thought this was really cool! My enthusiasm for it far outweighed his though, by a long shot. In fact, he complained that he really didn't want to do it at all and he was considering quitting. That didn't go over well with his father or me. We immediately broke into a long lecture about what an honor it is and how proud we were that he had been selected and under NO circumstances should he quit. Can you say "CONFLICT!"? After all, how could he ever be elected to Congress from the great state of Florida one day if he didn't want to hang with student council now? After we had a chance to collect our breaths, we compromised and he agreed to give it until the holidays to see if it would be something he would like. If not, he could quit. The holidays came and went and he stayed on student council.

There have been many things along these lines. Chad is good in sports, music, and other areas, but his pursuits of these things have to be his idea or he just won't fall in line. I do insist that he act responsibly and follow through with his commitments. Once he has seen his commitment through to it's agreed-upon end, it's his choice as to whether or not he continues. I have to work hard to keep my feelings in check, because I know that he can do anything he sets his mind to do. But, like most first born children (including his mother), he is strong-willed and stubborn and I find myself parking my expectations at the door much of the time. That is not to say that I let go of all my expectations — I do expect him to work up to his potential in school. I do expect for him to carry his weight in the household responsibilities (i.e. keeping his room clean, among other chores) and to participate in one extracurricular activity, which, right now, is Karate. Next year, he will begin guitar lessons, which is something we have all agreed to. There are so many other things I would like to expose him to, new experiences I want him to have, but those will hopefully come in time.

Most of all, I do not want unnecessary conflict with our son. There will be lessons he will have to learn on his own... the hard way... because that is the nature of the oldest child. That is fine, but it can be hard to stand by and watch him learn those lessons. When the doctor places your newborn baby in your arms for the first time, and you stare down into that sweet little face, you just know that you gave birth to THE perfect child and you dream wonderful dreams for what his/her life will become.

If I'm accused of this, I must confess, I am guilty as charged. I did this on a grand scale with all of my children, but particularly with Chad. My perfect son would never throw sand on the playground, smear a booger on the wall, or come home with less than perfect marks on his report card. Okay, reality does hit eventually and your perfect child does show his spots. But I've come to the conclusion that it is okay for children to learn things the hard way sometimes, as long as their physical and emotional safety is not threatened. As much as we would like to pave an easy way for our children, sometimes they have to find their own way and that can be a hard pill to swallow. But when we, as parents, can come to terms with the fact that it really IS okay, and there is no "perfect" child, life in the home becomes much happier. When you set the bar unrealistically high, sometimes your children learn how to limbo right under it and WHAM! They smack you over the head with your own stick! I'll admit, I have a lump or two on the cerebrum to prove it. I consider it a lesson learned.

The oldest child is stereotypically the "responsible one". This is true in our home. If you're lucky, part of being responsible means being the "keeper of the peace" amongst the siblings. More likely, it probably means "chief poobah tattle-taler." That is a double-edged sword. While it is helpful to have an informant on the "inside" (and oh so tempting to frequently tap into that source of information), I find it to be too easy to have a double standard. I want to know what is going on with my kids, but two minutes later, I'm admonishing them for being tattletales. It doesn't take kids long to pick up on this.

A View from the Parents' Corner

Answer this question quickly with the first thing that comes to mind—When you hear a thud, then a large crash in the next room, what's the first name you yell out? Did you say the name of your first child? That's how it is in our house. If he "did it", he's the first to catch the blame. If he didn't do it, he will know who did.

As I said before, I have special sympathy for our oldest son and try not to fall into negative traps while interacting with him. The teen years are swiftly approaching and I anticipate them with cautious optimism. At the tender age of 2, my beautiful oldest son dubbed me "the quitter of the fun" and I suppose I will hold that dubious title for many more years, particularly through the teen years. But my responsible, precious oldest son, who lives up to most every stereotype about the oldest child, is still the same sweet spirit that drubbled the words "love you, mommy" at 15 months of age and still wants me to tuck him in his bed every night. Every stage in the life of our oldest child is new for both him and for me. We learn our way through it together. Some days are easier than others and there's never a dull moment. But I treasure these days immensely, as I feel my little boy slipping away in favor of a young man. I hope this young man will understand that he always had my best efforts working on his behalf and my whole heart working toward his good. I will not "get it right" every time when dealing with him, but every effort I make will be made out of love. I hope he will always know that.

Our Joey

A View from the Parents' Corner

21. The Second Time Around: Joey

I wrote in the previous chapter about the sympathy I feel for Prince William of Britain. It's not easy being the oldest child. I will have to add that I feel a different kind of sympathy for Prince Harry. Being the second in line is no easy gig either. No matter what he accomplishes on his own, there will always be the inevitable comparisons to his older brother. I worried about these comparisons a lot when I became pregnant with my second child. I still worry about them to some degree today.

On a September morning in 1995, I awoke with a strange feeling. I was a little queasy and had not rested well the night before. "What is wrong with me?" I thought. I was really dragging my fanny that morning. I went downstairs to fix a bowl of cereal, but when I sat down to eat it, I realized that I couldn't; my stomach was too unsettled. This feeling was vaguely familiar and I looked up at the calender on my wall. The day before was circled and slowly it started dawning on me what could be wrong. I sent my husband to the drugstore up the street to buy a home pregnancy test. Within fifteen minutes, he was back with the test and waiting for me to take it. I hesitated. "Aren't you going to take it?" he asked. "No, I don't think so." I replied. "I'm going to give it one more day."

So, my husband left for work and I got on with the business of the morning. Thirteen month-old Chad and I played blocks, watched Barney, read books… and the curiosity was about to kill me. Still, I didn't want to waste a ten dollar pregnancy test when I probably wasn't pregnant. After all, we had so much trouble getting pregnant with Chad, we couldn't possibly be pregnant again so soon! By eleven that morning, I could wait no longer. I put Chad in his playpen, broke open the test and took the big dip... then waited, waited, waited for the full three minutes the directions said before I looked. Slowly, I picked up the test and there it was... two blue lines... PREGNANT! "Oh my!" I remember saying out loud.

I called David and he couldn't believe it, either. I walked around a little punch drunk for probably the next hour or so. Don't get me wrong, we were thrilled with the news; but there were complicating factors involved. I had been diagnosed with gall stones and was needing surgery to have my gall bladder removed. This new pregnancy was definitely going to make this situation more serious. After talking to my GYN, whose eyes rolled into the back of his head when he heard that I had become pregnant again before having the surgery, and with the gastroenterologist treating me, they determined that I would need to have the surgery despite the pregnancy due to the position of the stones in relationship to my pancreas. The only stipulation being that I would need the surgery sometime between weeks fourteen and eighteen of the pregnancy. I needed to be out of the first trimester for the sake of the baby's development, but not beyond the fifth month, at which time the position of the uterus would block access to the gall bladder.

As thrilled as I was about having another baby, I was afraid of potential negative effects of being operated on while pregnant. I was put on an ultra-low fat diet to keep my gall bladder from becoming further inflamed, and waited for the weeks to pass. I thought about this new baby constantly, and worried incessantly. Finally at

A View from the Parents' Corner

week fifteen, I was ready for surgery. The day before the scheduled surgery, I went in to my GYN for a routine visit and an ultrasound. It was my first look at Joey. His heart was beating strong and I had just begun to feel his kicks. I looked at him on the screen, this perfectly shaped little being. He stretched out an arm and I counted his fingers. At this point, we didn't know he was a boy, but I already knew that I loved him. He was as real to me as my little boy at home, and I was scared to death for him and me.

The night before my surgery I didn't sleep. I paced nervously around the house until time to leave for the hospital. When I arrived at the hospital, my nerves finally got the best of me. I drug my I.V. pole into the bathroom and got sick... really sick. Fortunately, I had not had anything to eat since the day before, so a shot of Phenagren settled my stomach rather quickly. The nurse came in and told me I was next to go back, and put a sedative into my line. "I don't want to go to sleep now" I told her. "I need to talk to Dr. Bobo." (my surgeon) I felt the effects of the drug almost immediately, but I fought the urge to sleep. Finally I was wheeled into the operating room, where my surgeon and his team were waiting. Dr. Bobo was dressed in scrubs with a mask already covering his face. I mumbled to him and he bent down close to my face for me to repeat what I said. "I am afraid" I managed to say. "You and your baby are going to be just fine" he re-assured me. He then announced to the surgical team in there that I was fifteen weeks pregnant. A momentary hush came over the room, then one of the nurses bent down over me and said "Congratulations!"

"We'll be ready to start in just a minute, Laura." Dr. Bobo said. I just nodded and closed my eyes and said a prayer.

I prayed for God to guide the hands of this team and to take care of my baby. The anesthesiologist came over with a mask and was ready to put me out. "Wait!" I said. "I'm not ready!" Dr. Bobo leaned over. "What's wrong, Laura?" he asked. I remember turning my head and looking at him straight in the eye, despite being sedated, and saying "Please take care of my baby, I already love him." "We will, Laura, we will monitor him the whole time" he said. With that being said, the mask was placed on my face and I started counting backwards... ten, nine, eight... and then there was darkness.

"Laura, wake up, you are in recovery... Laura, are you awake?" the voice repeated. I was awake. I could hear my name being called but I had not yet opened my eyes. I felt pain shooting through my stomach and I groaned. Immediately I felt a nurse putting something into my line and within moments, the pain subsided. I still would not open my eyes; I tried, but the light in the room was too bright. I mumbled "The baby...", but that's all I could say. My throat was sore from the breathing tube that had been inserted during the surgery. "Laura, it's Dr. Bonk (one of the OB's in the office). You and the baby did just fine. Would you like to hear your baby's heart beating?" I managed to mumble "Yes", and I felt a pair of headphones being placed on my ears. Within moments, I could hear my baby's heart beating strongly and a great sense of relief swept over me. It took hours for the sedation to wear off, but I knew that everything had gone well.

Later that night, my surgeon came by the hospital room carrying a jar full of gall stones. "Just thought you might like to see what was causing all the trouble" he said as he placed the jar on my tray next to the bed. After seeing those rocks, I could see why I had been in so much pain. I thanked him over and over for taking good care of us. I heard many months later, well after Joey was born, that every time Dr. Bobo ran into my OB at the hospital, he always asked how my baby and I were doing. I thought it was very sweet that he took a personal interest in our well-being.

After a few weeks' recovery time, life returned to normal. At nineteen weeks, I went in for a follow-up ultrasound. I knew that it was likely that we would find out the sex of the baby at this appointment. People had asked me if I wanted a boy or girl. I always said that it didn't matter. Secretly, in my heart, I very much wanted another boy. When I pictured the baby in my mind, I always thought of two little brothers playing on the floor. Of course, we would not have been at all disappointed with a girl, but something in my mind was thinking "boy".

Once it was confirmed that we were having another boy, I knew right away what I wanted to name him. "Joey" had always been one of my favorite boy names. I would probably have chosen to use that name with the first child if I could have convinced David. David was concerned that "Joey" might sound too babyish once he was a teenager and might cause him to be teased at school. We agreed that when he was middle school age, that we would call him "Joe". He is getting close to that age now, and if he wants to go by "Joe" we certainly will, but he will always be my Joey.

As I was approaching the end of my pregnancy, I began to have very mixed feelings about what was about to happen to the family dynamics in our home. I was absolutely thrilled to be having another son, but in some ways my excitement made me feel very disloyal to Chad. There is only 22 months age difference between the boys, and he didn't have a clue about what was getting ready to happen in our home. Little did he know that a "little intruder" was getting ready to sneak into our lives and steal his mommy away. How was I going to be able to show all the love I felt for Joey without it taking away from Chad? This was a question I worried about and had no answer to. I already loved Joey, but I couldn't comprehend how I could love anyone else the way that I loved Chad. I worried and fretted. I knew that I would, but I just didn't know HOW.

At 38 1/2 weeks, my doctors decided that due to my rapid labor with Chad, that I would be induced. I was dilated to 3 cm, but was not showing signs of active labor. Upon admission to the hospital, I began my obligatory walks up and down the halls to try to start labor. After a few hours of no progression, the Pitocin was brought in. That is bad stuff! I had not been on the Pitocin very long when active labor began. I hollered at my nurse to go find that anesthesiologist pronto... I had no intentions of going through natural childbirth again. "Dr. Feelgood" arrived just in time to save my sanity and to get that epidural on board. The epidural was no picnic itself, but once it took, I was in no pain; I was downright giddy. "I'm going to get a little sleep," I said and the nurse turned off the light. About an hour later, my nurse came in and told me it was time to push... I didn't even know I was close to delivery; I couldn't feel a thing. I had a hard time pushing with Joey. I was so numb from the epidural that I couldn't bear down.

Finally, after half an hour, Joseph Patrick Hull was born at

A View from the Parents' Corner

3:02 am. He was not happy! He wailed at the top of his lungs and promptly peed on the doctor in defiance. This was a sharp contrast to the entrance his brother had made less than two years earlier. When Chad was born, he came out calm, just looking around, taking it all in. The doctor literally had to give him several little spanks to make him cry in order to clear his lungs. Joey, on the other hand, made it clear that he was not at all pleased to be taken out of the nice warm home of his mother's body, in favor of bright lights and loud noises. These two boys had different temperaments coming out of the box. I need to look no further than their presentations upon delivery to illustrate this. It is still true to this day.

When the doctor handed Joey to me, he looked nothing like Chad. His facial features bore a strong resemblance to mine. I just looked down at him as he studied my face and my heart was full of love for my precious little boy. How silly it had been for me to be worried about "how" I would love him as much as Chad. The fact was "I just did." I kissed his beautiful little face softly and told him I was his mommy and I would always love him. I sang "I Love You a Bushel and a Peck" to him. I nursed Joey for 45 minutes before he was taken to the nursery. Once I was cleaned up, I was transported to my private room, where I slept well, knowing that all the uncertainty I had felt was unnecessary. My sweet Joey had a place in my heart, all of his own, and it didn't take anything away from how I felt about Chad.

Chad adjusted well to his new brother. I would still stop and sing the Barney "I love you" song (a.k.a. "our song") with him whenever it was on, and I wore myself out trying to spend extra time with Chad whenever Joey slept. During that first year, I never really had any relief from the profound fatigue that goes along with having a new baby. The first year with both boys was wonderful, but physically brutal. I was breastfeeding Joey and potty-training Chad and I rarely left the house. It was during that year that my body somehow adjusted to functioning on a lot less sleep. Even to this day, I rarely sleep more than seven hours.

Even though the first year was hard with having the boys so close in age, I have found that as they have gotten older the age difference has been very positive. They are good company to each other and have many of the same interests. I look back at those days sometimes and wonder where all the time has gone and wonder how we survived it. It is amazing how well we can adjust to the stresses in our lives when our hearts are leading the efforts.

Fortunately, Chad and Joey are as different as night and day. Because they are so different, I think this has helped stave off comparisons between the two boys. Chad acts and looks more like David. Joey favors me in many respects. I had worried about Joey coming "second in line" behind Chad, but so far, this has not been a big issue in our home. Even though in many respects Chad is a hard act to follow, Joey shines just as brightly in his own way, and I hope neither of our sons will feel competitive with the other or feel that he doesn't "measure up". Each child brings his own strengths to the table, and I know it will always be that way. Everyone's place in our home is special and irreplaceable, no matter where they fall in the birth order.

A View from the Parents' Corner

22. Battling Lupus: The Birth Of Laurie

After the birth of Joey, the jump from one to two children was a difficult transition and we were slow to make plans for baby number three. Deep in my heart, I had always dreamed of having a little girl, and I was so ready to dress up a little baby in pink and lace. Shortly after Joey's second birthday, we were ready to try again. In the summer of 1998, I became pregnant for the third time... the first month we tried. Because we were looking for the pregnancy, I tested the first day I was late and knew very early that we were expecting again. Within a few days however, I began spotting and miscarried within the week. Had I not been looking for the pregnancy, I would have probably never known I was pregnant. Anytime a woman has a miscarriage, doctors advise waiting two cycles to become pregnant again. So, we waited through the summer before trying again. By October, we were pregnant again.

Everything seemed to be fine with this pregnancy in the beginning. I was having all the early signs of pregnancy — queasiness, bloating, frequent urination, fatigue — every indicator was that the pregnancy was progressing normally. However, at the beginning of week seven, I woke up in the middle of the night to go to the bathroom and realized I was spotting. My heart sank as I went back to bed. I considered calling my doctor, but I knew that he would just tell me to go to bed and stay off my feet. I went back to bed, but couldn't get back to sleep.

I went to my OB's office the next day. I laid on the table as the ultrasound tech scanned my pelvic area. There I saw my baby... the little heart beating on the screen, but the tech was quiet as she measured and scanned. "Does everything look okay?" I asked her. "I can't really say for sure. The doctor will have to look at the pictures." After dressing, I waited in the doctor's office for him to come in to speak to me. Dr. Davis was not in the office that day, so I had to speak with one of the other doctors in the office. "You are not measuring out at seven weeks, Mrs. Hull", the doctor began, "which means one of two things... either your dates were wrong and you are not as far along as we thought, or you are at the beginning of a miscarriage." I knew that my dates were correct, and realized that the pregnancy was not progressing normally. I was told to go on complete bed rest to see if the bleeding would stop. Even though the thought of losing this baby was disheartening, the thought of a baby developing with potential problems was downright frightening. I went on complete bed rest, but my bleeding increased over the next several days, and at eight weeks, I had another miscarriage. David and I were both heartbroken, and did not know if we were would be willing to go through another potential disappointment.

I had a gut feeling that something was wrong with me medically. It just did not make sense to me that after having two relatively healthy pregnancies, that I would have two back-to-back miscarriages. Fortunately, I had a wonderful doctor in Dr. Davis, who agreed with me that something could be wrong. The testing done on the embryo I had miscarried indicated no abnormalities, and so the problem appeared to be with me. Dr. Davis ordered a truckload of blood work, shooting in the dark for a possible reason for my miscarriages. The second set of labs revealed something unexpected and devastating. At the age of 28, I was diagnosed with lupus.

Even though I was chronically tired and prone to illness, I was caught completely off guard by my diagnosis. Upon receiving my test results, I was referred to a rheumatologist, who would follow and treat my lupus. I have a form of lupus that deals with the blood's ability to clot. My condition, called "Anti-phospholipid syndrome" is particularly a problem during pregnancy. My body develops antibodies against the baby and the baby's placenta, eventually destroying both. This condition has an eighty percent failure rate for pregnancies, if not treated aggressively. It's also dangerous to me because during pregnancy, my blood is too thick and it makes me very prone to blood clots. My rheumatologist advised me to be thankful for the two children I had and to not even consider becoming pregnant again. I was heartbroken. I was racked with guilt over a healthy baby that my body had destroyed and I felt extreme sadness over a dream slipping away. I thought of the little girl I would never have, and I wondered if the baby I had just lost was the little girl I had always dreamed of having. Even more than this, I worried about a disease that might rob me of seeing my boys grow up.

Everything I read about lupus scared me. I worried about my health deteriorating; I worried about my ability to take care of my children. I laid awake at night and sweated thinking about what could happen in a worst case scenario. I worried about what would happen to my family if I weren't around. I tried not to show how scared I actually was. I always downplayed my fears about the disease when David and I talked about it. I didn't see how it would help to have him worried, too. In thinking back on it now, I realize that on those nights when I was lying there awake, overcome with fear, I should have awakened him and shared my feelings and my fears. We both had a lot to lose, and it was wrong for me to withhold my feelings from him.

Within a two week period, I miscarried a baby that we very much wanted and I was diagnosed with lupus. My heart was on the floor and I was consumed with sadness. I knew I needed to resume "life as usual" or I was going to fall into depression. Lupus is a disease that can usually be managed, but there's no "cure". With little control over this aspect of my life, I concluded that I needed to just live my life to the fullest of my ability, and not wring my hands over what I couldn't change. I didn't want our lives to be defined by my illness. I knew I would never have the same health again, but with proper care, I could live a very normal life. That's what I've done.

Exactly four weeks after my second miscarriage, toward the end of November, I started showing signs of pregnancy again. At first my doctor thought that I had some remnants of the old pregnancy still in my uterus and that I would need a DNC to rid my body of the remains of the pregnancy. However, blood work showed that this was in fact, a new pregnancy. I had gotten pregnant just two weeks after the miscarriage. I'll admit straight up — it didn't occur to me that I could get pregnant that quickly on the heels of a miscarriage. There was only one night when we didn't take precautions, and that was apparently the night I became pregnant again. When the new pregnancy was confirmed late that afternoon, I immediately went home and called my rheumatologist. My doctor was in with patients and I left a message with his nurse: "Please tell him that Laura Hull is pregnant again. What do I need to do?" It was roughly 4:00 in the afternoon when I left the message, so I was not expecting to hear from him that day. At 8:00 pm that night, my phone rang and it was my doctor calling me from his home. He wasn't happy with me. After reminding me that this presented a potentially dangerous situation for me and the baby, he asked me if I would consider a therapeutic abortion. I told him absolutely not. He advised me to be at his office at 8:00 the next morning so that we could sit down and map out a plan for managing the pregnancy.

Bright and early the next day, I sat down with Dr. Botstein, my rheumatologist, and after consulting with a maternal/fetal medicine group in town, it was decided I would start on steroids and aspirin to control the lupus and to keep my blood thin. I would need monthly ultrasounds to make sure the baby's growth was normal and to watch the heart develop, since women with lupus sometimes have babies with heart defects.

I knew I was going to need a new OB. Dr. Davis was set to retire midway through my pregnancy. A friend recommended Dr. Pam Brown, who was a member of our large church. Although I didn't know her personally at this point, I had heard good things about her, and I needed someone good, quickly. Using a copy of our church directory, I called her at home and ask if she would be interested in helping me. My end of the conversation went something like this... "Hi! You don't know me, but we go to church together. My name is Laura Hull. I have lupus. I just found out I'm pregnant... would you be willing to help me... would you be my doctor?" Looking back on it, I really put Pam on the spot. This was a risky pregnancy, with a lot of uncertainty attached. I asked her to take responsibility for me and my baby, knowing that she would have to see me at church every week, even if we had a bad outcome. But Pam was great—she agreed to take me as her patient, and provided me with excellent care.

Bleeding problems started almost immediately. Even though ultrasounds showed that everything appeared to be progressing normally, I started spotting again very early. This required me to increase my steroids. I had almost resigned myself to the fact that I was probably going to miscarry again. On December 23, I went in to the OB's office to have some blood work drawn, to measure my hormone levels to see if the pregnancy was still healthy. But by the close of the business day on December 24, my blood work had still not come back, so I was forced to wait through Christmas to find out if our baby was okay. Bright and early on Christmas morning, our two boys ran into our room and woke us up around 7:00 am to see what treasures Santa had brought the night before. David and I were both caught up in the excitement of the morning, when our telephone rang around 7:30... it was Pam. She had gone into her office, on Christmas morning, to retrieve my test results which had come over the fax machine on Christmas Eve after her office closed. She called to tell me that my blood work looked great and that my pregnancy was healthy. The steroids were working and the bleeding was probably just implantation bleeding and of no significance. That was probably the best Christmas gift I have ever received! I was so blown away that Pam would have left her home on Christmas morning to go to her office to find my test results so that I could have a joyous Christmas. My heart was touched and it was then that I knew that Pam was not only my doctor, but my friend. Over the next several months, we did develop a friendship. We have children the same ages, who became friends as well. It has never felt strange to me that Pam was my doctor, who became my friend. I was just relieved that I had someone taking care of me who was invested in me, not only as her patient, but as her friend. We are still friends to this day, and we make a point to see each other every time my family visits Georgia.

My pregnancy progressed normally. The steroids aggravated my morning sickness and made it hard to sleep, but it was allowing our baby and me to live, so I didn't mind the side effects too much. I was beginning to settle in with the fact that the pregnancy would most likely be fine, so we started to think about names. We settled on a boy's name rather quickly (Bailey) but we struggled with a girl's name. One afternoon, I was going through an old box of letters, cards, and keepsakes that I had not gone through in years. In that box, I ran across a valentine card that was dated February 14, 1975. It was a card my grandmother had sent to me that simply said "I love you, Laurie." My grandmother, who I loved dearly, was the only person in my life who ever called me "Laurie" and somehow, I had forgotten that. Seeing that message, in my grandmother's own handwriting (she had passed away in 1986) struck a cord in my heart. It was as if my grandmother were whispering into my ear and into my heart. Suddenly, I knew what we would name our daughter. If I had a girl, she would be named Laura, and we would call her "Laurie". Her middle name would be "Diana" after my mother. Laura Diana Hull... "Laurie"; it just felt right.

At fourteen weeks, my maternal/fetal medicine doctor, who was working with Pam on my case, conducted what I thought was going to be just a routine ultrasound. He scanned my belly for a moment. Everything looked great. Then he said, "I can see the sex of the baby. Do you want to know what you are having?" It hadn't occurred to me that he would be able to see the sex of the baby so early. David wasn't even with me, since this was just supposed to be a quick scan. "Don't tell me unless you know for sure." I said. He uttered the words I will never forget, "Would you be very disappointed, Laura, if I told you that your third child is a girl?" Of course, he was asking this in jest. Everyone who was working on my case knew how much I wanted a girl. "Are you sure?" I asked. "I give you my nursery guarantee... if I am wrong about the sex of the baby, I'll pay to have the wallpaper in your nursery changed." I could not hide the exhilaration I was feeling. "It's a girl! I can't believe I'm having a girl!" I thought to myself... and my smile was a mile wide. I must have floated out of the exam room... my feet never touched the ground. I couldn't contain my excitement. "I'm having a girl!" I said to everyone I passed on the way out.

I stopped by my parents' house on the way home to pick up my boys. I beamed as I held up my ultrasound pictures and declared, "I want to show you a picture of our daughter, Laurie!" and that's how I broke the news that we were having a little girl. David just chuckled. "A little girl!? What do you do for little girls?" He didn't know what to think about the prospect of years of baby dolls and frilly pink tutus. I assured him that when the time came, he'd be just as into those things as he was into the boys' things.

A View from the Parents' Corner

At twenty weeks of pregnancy, my husband accepted a job in Saint Petersburg, Florida. My pregnancy was stable and we took advantage of a move that was good overall for our family. I immediately sought out the maternal/fetal medicine group in St. Pete to take over my case. I liked all three doctors in the group, but Dr. Raimer was my favorite. She was the mother of a large brood herself, and I generally like female doctors better, anyway.

At thirty weeks, I began having side effects from long term steroid use. My face and hands were swelling badly and I was feeling a little crazy. It finally got to the point where I told Dr. Raimer at one visit "I'll be lucky to get out of this pregnancy without being divorced by my husband, disowned by my parents, and dumped by my friends..." The steroids were making me mean. I could always keep it in check with my boys — I never lost my temper with them — but everyone else had better watch out. Long term steroid use really messes with your emotions, particularly in terms of anger management. You can know that your feelings are way out of proportion to the situation, but you can't help the feelings any more than you can help breathing. I am just lucky that my husband, parents, and friends understood I was struggling with the effects of my medication and didn't hold my bad attitude against me.

In the final weeks of my pregnancy, I rushed to finish Laurie's nursery. It was fun to do a room in pink. I had a ball shopping for all new girl things. I packed a pretty pink dress, a pink blanket, and a pink hair bow into my suitcase to bring her home from the hospital. I couldn't wait to meet my daughter; to hold her in my arms. At thirty eight weeks, following another quick labor, our beautiful Laurie was born. After she was placed in my arms, I remember unwrapping her blanket to look at her. I couldn't believe she was real. I was completely in love with her. Here she was... the daughter I had always dreamed of... a dream that almost eluded us. All the months of uncertainty, all the months of sickness and steroid use... it was so worth it. She was perfect in every way; her heart was normal and she showed no ill affects from my long-term steroid use. She was so beautiful... I could not believe how beautiful she was. I couldn't get over how much she looked like David! Her resemblance to David was so strong it looked like he had cloned himself. (except in the diaper area!) And oh my! David found out quite quickly what little girls do — little girls wrap their daddies around their little fingers! Watching David with Laurie was heartwarming; he was holding his little princess and she had him by his heart.

My little Laurie... my Laurie girl, was everything I dreamed she would be. I made up a little song that I would sing to her in the middle of the night, "Hey there, Laurie girl" sung to the tune of "Georgie Girl". I would just look down at her and think about all the wonderful girl things we would do together as she grew older, all the things we would share between us. I was looking forward to the experience of raising a daughter, and wondered how it would differ from raising my boys. I felt so blessed that I was given the opportunity to experience the thrill of raising both boys and a girl. I was so grateful to the wonderful doctors who had taken such good care of us. But mostly I just had to thank God for watching over us and delivering Laurie into our lives safely. Fortunately, the pregnancy didn't cause my lupus to progress and my health remained stable following the pregnancy. Whether or not future pregnancies would be possible would have to be evaluated as time passed and my lupus status was monitored.

Laurie made her own place in our home very quickly. Chad and Joey were both thrilled to have a little sister and were very gentle and protective of her. Laurie was a very calm baby; she didn't cry very much. She was an easy baby, much like Chad had been. She was certainly the little princess in our home and she still holds that title today. Laurie is everything I could have ever hoped for and dreamed of in a daughter. I look forward to the wonderful experiences that we will undoubtedly share down the road. Laurie is living proof for me that with a little bit of patience and endurance, and a whole lotta faith, hope and love... sometimes dreams really do come true.

Our Laurie

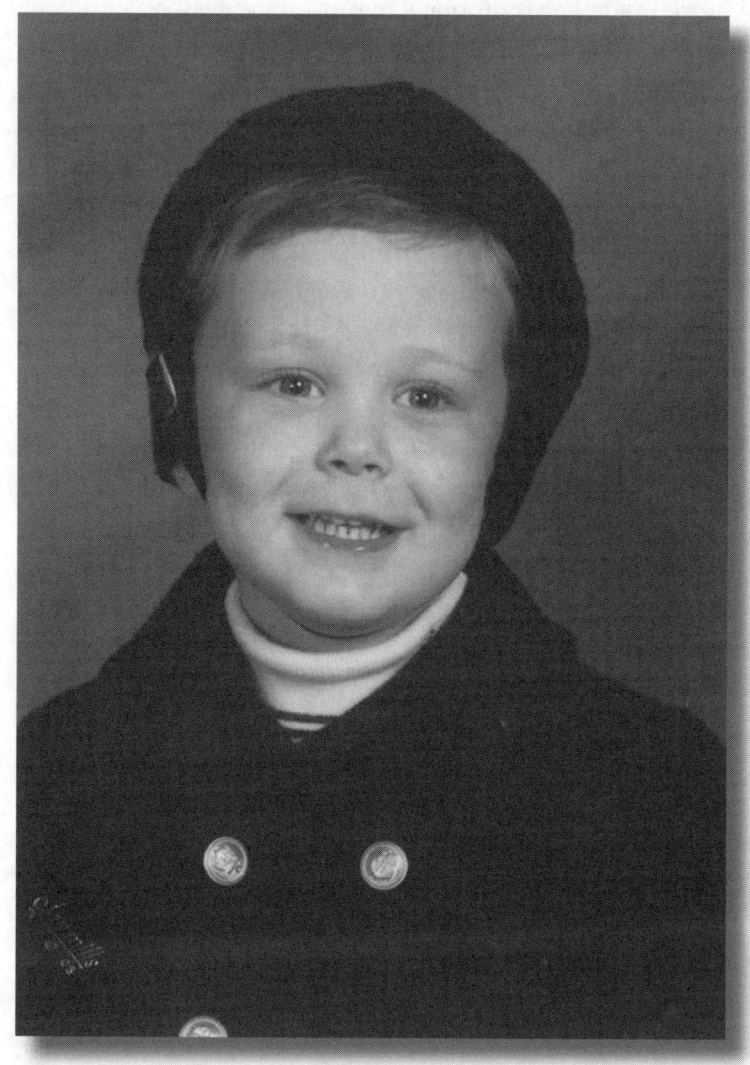

Our Zach

23. Our Little Venetian Baby: Zach

Zach is our fourth child. The story of his arrival on the scene is a wild one. In the spring of 2001, our entire family took a month-long trip to Europe. It was a wonderful trip, filled with special memories. Early in our trip we made a two day stop in Venice, Italy. Oh, Venice... now that is a romantic city. Never mind the fact that we had our three young children with us on this trip... David and I still felt a hint of romance as we strolled through the city... a little sweet talking and a little "over the kids' heads" flirting between the two of us. I won't elaborate too much, but let's just say that we did find a moment during that stop in Venice to appreciate the romantic mood of the city. Actually, it was the only romantic moment on that whole trip, if you get my drift.

After visiting five countries during that trip, we returned home elated from the amazing things we saw and experienced, but we were absolutely drained physically. My rheumatologist, Dr. Milord, isn't really in favor of the kind of extensive traveling that we like to do. Traveling overseas, with jet lag and at times poor nutrition, is especially hard on people with lupus. Inevitably, after returning from a trip like this, I experience a brief flare-up of my auto-immune disease, which is quickly brought under control by rest, good nutrition, and a short-term round of oral steroids.

The first several days after returning home, I was experiencing the symptoms of a flare-up... fatigue, muscle and joint pain, occasional dizziness. The symptoms I was experiencing seemed to be markedly worse than ever before. I called my rheumatologist's office and was prescribed a week's worth of steroids to help me get through the flare-up and was advised to rest. The next few days passed uneventfully, but I wasn't feeling better. I was feeling worse and was beginning to have stomach problems on top of the jet lag and lupus symptoms. Finally, after an afternoon nap, a week after our return from Europe, I went to the bathroom and was having breakthrough bleeding. The only times I had ever had breakthrough bleeding in my life was when I was pregnant. Thinking about where I was in my monthly cycle, it hit me: the night in Venice!

I sent David scrambling once again to the drug store. The pregnancy test confirmed I was carrying a little Venetian baby! I have to admit, I was a little embarrassed to call my rheumatologist that afternoon to say "Guess what? One starry night and a gondola ride in Venice and here comes baby number four!" I was advised to continue with the steroids and to come into the office the next day. I also called my maternal/fetal medicine group to alert them to the fact that I had a positive home pregnancy test, and an ultrasound the next day confirmed that we were definitely expecting again.

All of our friends and family seemed to take note that we must have conceived this baby while we were in Europe. "Weren't your kids in the room with you the whole trip? How did you guys pull that one off?" was asked by a few friends. (The answer to that question: very, very quietly!) I had to be honest with my doctors concerning the conception of Zach. They needed to understand why I was in such bad shape physically (from the trip, and the subsequent flare-up of my lupus). I took a lot of ribbing from the nurses in my OB's office. Word had circulated around the office about our little European souvenir. An ultrasound tech in the office named Sue, nicknamed the baby "Giacomo", and that nickname stuck throughout my pregnancy.

Everything seemed normal with the pregnancy, but I was not in good health. Starting a new pregnancy in the middle of a lupus flare up is not a good thing. Pregnancy is hard on the body of a healthy woman. It's extremely hard on the body of a woman whose body is being compromised by lupus. My body struggled to adjust to the new pregnancy and the increased steroid use. My doctors decided to follow the same medical protocol with this pregnancy as I had in my pregnancy with Laurie. It had worked well before, and there was no reason to think that it wouldn't work again. However, there was one major difference between my pregnancy with Laurie and this new one. This time, I was in the worst health of my life. I was unable to regain my strength from the trip due to the pregnancy, and my lupus symptoms were raging.

One evening, at twelve weeks of pregnancy, I experienced an episode that sent me to the emergency room. I was experiencing profound exhaustion and pain when breathing. Both my OB and rheumatologist told me to go to the emergency room immediately, where a blood test revealed a problem. A test called a "D-Dimer" revealed that my blood was too thick, and that I most likely had a blood clot somewhere in my body, probably the lungs. A chest x-ray proved inconclusive. My doctors wanted to do a nuclear lung scan to confirm the clot. "Is that test safe for the baby?" I asked the doctor treating me in the emergency room. I was looking for re-assurance, but in all honesty he could not say that the baby would be unaffected. "Then I won't consent to the test!" I said. The doctor urged me to reconsider, but I told him just to treat me as he would if he had confirmation of a clot. He grew rather impatient with me. I'm sure he felt I was being unwise, but I couldn't settle in with doing a test that could potentially harm the development of our child.

The doctor treating me then left my exam room to call my OB and rheumatologist to inform them of my decision about the test, and to consult with them on my treatment. I laid there alone in that exam room for what seemed like hours. David was with our other children at that time, and the reality of my situation came crashing in on me during my time alone. I knew I needed to reach thirty six weeks of pregnancy to ensure the baby's safety, but I was only at week twelve and already having serious complications. My rheumatologist had started saying things along the lines of "we really need to get you to twenty nine weeks; thirty two would be even better." This told me that they weren't sure about my ability to carry this pregnancy to term. The thought of delivering a baby too early scared me. I knew that we needed to get to at least thirty four weeks; thirty six being even better. But thirty six weeks seemed like a long way away. A blood clot in the lungs can be fatal and I was scared to death. I thought of my three beautiful children at home who needed their mother, and I felt very selfish for putting them in a position where they could potentially have to grow up without me. Don't get me wrong... we very much wanted this baby I was carrying, but it wasn't exactly smart to get pregnant in this set of circumstances. In that moment I felt stupid... careless and stupid.

Eventually, my emergency room physician returned and I was admitted to the hospital for treatment. My rheumatologist scolded me for putting myself in jeopardy by getting pregnant the way I did. She let me know in no uncertain terms that she felt we had been foolish. She was giving me a good kick in the pants, but she had to move over while everyone else who cared about us took a turn with the boot. Even though a big part of me wanted this baby desperately, I knew that my health and the life of my baby was in peril. I was very torn up inside with feelings that left me with constant inner turmoil. Over the next few days, I underwent more testing and was monitored carefully as the doctors watched how my body responded to treatment. My steroid levels were doubled and in a few days, I was allowed to go home. My body responded appropriately to the increased steroid levels and my D-Dimer levels soon returned to the normal range. The immediate threat was over, but the increased steroid use over a long period of time eventually presented problems of its own.

Shortly after my release from the hospital, I had another ultrasound, at roughly thirteen weeks. As with all of my boys, our baby was not shy about showing the family jewels and we found out that we were having another little boy. Of course, the sex of the baby was not a huge issue for David and me. We were far more concerned with just having a healthy baby. However, amongst our children, the addition of another boy provoked a mixed response. Laurie, of course, was hoping for a little sister, and Joey was lobbying hard for another brother. Chad, on the other hand, very much wanted another sister, (at this point, Chad thought that sisters did not get "into your stuff" like little brothers, eg: Joey) and he was quite upset that Joey had "gotten his way" on this issue.

David and I had not settled on a boy name at this point, so we told Chad he would be allowed to choose a name for the baby and that if everyone liked it, we would name his brother the name he had chosen. This seemed to smooth over the whole brother/sister issue. It didn't take Chad long to come up with a name: he liked the name "Zach". Chad liked this name because there was a very talented kid in his karate class named Zach who every one called "The Zach Attack". Chad thought that was a cool name and Zach was his choice for the baby's name. Truthfully, Zach was not a name I had ever considered. But everyone seemed to like it, so we decided to go with it. Chad was very proud that he had been given the task of naming his new brother, and I thought he had made a really good choice. I just needed to find a good middle name to go with it. In search of a middle name, I resorted to thumbing through a baby name book. I wanted to choose something a little different. I figured there were enough Justins and Joshuas in the world. I finally ran across one name that caught my attention: Dawson. The name Dawson means "David's son". I thought that was a special name, mostly for its meaning, and by my fourth month of pregnancy, we had settled on the name "Zachary Dawson Hull".

By the beginning of the third trimester, my body was starting to show signs of steroid overuse. I was swelling badly. The swelling in my feet and ankles was so bad that I could actually feel the fluid "swishing" in my feet as I walked. My legs began to spontaneously bruise from the pressure of the fluid. At this point my blood pressure was not a problem, but I began to experience lupus-induced problems with my eyes. One day while driving home from picking up my boys at school, I was having trouble seeing. Despite wearing dark sunglasses, the light reflecting off of the cars in front of me was burning my eyes. I was able to make it home, but I knew something was wrong with my eyes. I called my rheumatologist who instructed me to see an ophthalmologist immediately. The ophthalmologist who saw me diagnosed me with lupus-induced iritis. Basically, my body was forming antibodies to the irises in my eyes. The answer to the problem: more steroids. I was falling apart.

At thirty two weeks, I was put on bed rest when an ultrasound showed that Zach's amniotic fluid levels were too low... a side effect from long-term steroid use. I never had this with Laurie and don't know why it was a problem with Zach. I was ordered to drink 120 oz of water per day and to stay in bed. Unfortunately, the amniotic fluid levels would not stay consistently normal, and the decision was made at thirty six weeks to induce labor. Because my fluid levels were so low, they were unable to perform an amniocentesis to check for lung maturity. We did not know if Zach was ready to be born. But my doctors thought the risk of a cord accident was too great and the decision was made to go on with the premature delivery.

It took two days to deliver Zach. My body was no where near ready for labor and it was a long, painful process to get him delivered. I was pumped full of I.V. steroids and antibiotics over those two days and I had very little rest or food during that time. Finally on the morning of January 11, at 11:25 am, our beautiful Zach was born. When I got my first look at him, I was amazed at how beautiful he was, and I was frightened at how small he looked. "Do you think he even weighs six pounds?" I asked my doctor.

"I don't know..." he answered. "He's a little guy."

Because Zach was premature, he was not handed to me immediately after he was born. He was taken to the incubator where two nurses conducted his APGAR. I nervously watched as they monitored him and I listened for his cry. He sounded healthy to me. "What's his APGAR?" I asked the nurses. "Perfect ten!" the nurse said with a smile. A few moments later, the nurse wrapped Zach up in warm blankets and brought him over to me. He was so beautiful. He looked like a perfect blend of Chad and Joey. I was so relieved to hold him in my arms. I thought back to the last time I had been in the hospital at twelve weeks and couldn't believe we had made it all the way down that long road. I felt like I'd climbed Mount Everest and was standing at the summit, with my fist pumped in the air. We'd made it! We'd made it and everyone was fine! We had a birthday party, complete with cake and balloons, for our little Zach that night, as the family celebrated his birth. Other than being a little small, Zach was perfectly healthy and showed no signs of problems from his premature birth.

After delivering Zach, I developed post-delivery pre-eclampsia. My blood pressure shot up to 180/110 and my face was so distorted from swelling that to this day, I won't look at the photographs of me taken during those early days following Zach's birth. After two weeks of bed rest, blood pressure medication, and diuretics, my condition stabilized. It was determined that my body had built up some type of intolerance to the steroids, which had caused the amniotic fluid level problems and my post delivery blood pressure problems. I was probably not going to be able to be on long-term steroids again. My body just can't tolerate them. It was at this point that we conceded that

A View from the Parents' Corner

our family was probably complete. Unless there was an alternative to steroids during pregnancy for treating my lupus, we wouldn't be having any more children.

After all the "scary stuff" went away, I was able to enjoy my little Zachy. He had so much personality, and a wonderful smile. He was a voracious eater; he quickly gained weight and made up for the fact that he was small at birth. I made up a little song for him called "Zach, My Doodle Doo", which I still sing to him. (Don't look for it in the CD section of your favorite music store, it's a Laura Hull original)

I had almost forgotten how nice it was to have a little boy again. I pictured in my mind my little Zach around the age of six or seven, out in the yard, pitching a ball with his two older brothers. I thought of how special it would be for him to have two such wonderful older brothers as role models. I thought of my little Laurie, who in being sandwiched between three brothers would probably never be allowed to date! My heart was full of love for this sweet little boy, and all of the physical and emotional stress of the pregnancy faded as Zach made his own place in our home and in our hearts.

Eventually, my health stabilized and my lupus went back into remission. Even though the pregnancy was risky, I cannot honestly say that I have regrets. I guess that is easy to say because we had a good outcome. But as I said earlier, I do not believe in accidents in this life, and I know that our precious Zach was meant to be here with us. I cannot picture my life without him. I look back at what my family and I had to endure in order to bring Zach safely into the world, and it brings to mind a wonderful quote by Toby Devens Schwartz with which I will close. It conveys my feelings exactly: "Happy is the woman who holds her child to the light and says 'it was worth it. It was worth it, Lord, thank you.'"

24. And Baby Makes Seven: The Birth Of Lanie

After Zach was born, we knew it would be highly unlikely that we would have any more children. Even though we still had the desire for more children, my pregnancy and post delivery with Zach had been dangerous enough for us to consider our family complete. I always wished that Laurie would have the opportunity to grow up with a sister. But it didn't look like that was going to be possible.

On a Wednesday morning in June of 2003, I woke up feeling really BAD... Stomach sick, pale, and head pounding. I was a few days late and my symptoms certainly mimicked morning sickness, but I didn't give much thought to the possibility that I could be pregnant again. As the day wore on, the symptoms would not subside and I was so fatigued that I could hardly get off of the couch. I had no fever, but was pretty sure that I either had a stomach virus or a mild case of food poisoning. I managed to pull it together during the late afternoon to take my kids to swim team practice, but the heat of being at the pool made my sick stomach feel even worse. All day long I kept asking my kids, "Do you feel okay? Does your stomach hurt?" in case we had a bug going through the house. But everyone was fine, except for me.

On the way home from swim team, I had to stop at the store to pick up a few things for dinner. I walked down the medicine isle and passed by the home pregnancy tests. I picked up one quickly and threw it in the cart without my children noticing. As long as the test came back negative, I intended to medicate myself heavily after preparing dinner for the rest of my family, and go to bed to sleep off my illness.

As dinner was simmering on the stove, I made my way to the bathroom and began to dry heave. "Oh, this is bad" I remember uttering out loud. I took the pregnancy test out of the box, urinated into a cup, took the big dip, and brought the test stick into the kitchen with me while I attended to the dinner on the stove. Three minutes later, I read the test results, which showed two pink lines... pregnant! I remember picking up the stick, seeing the results and literally stumbling backwards into a kitchen chair behind me as the reality of the results sunk in. I was completely shocked.

I waited until the next day to tell David the news. Even though we were both thrilled at the thought of having another baby, the reality of my medical situation was daunting. A new pregnancy had risks, significant risks involved and those could not just be overlooked.

I called my maternal/fetal medicine group the next day and was worked in for an ultrasound. Everything looked normal on the ultrasound and the decision was made that day to forgo steroid treatments in favor of a low-molecular weight form of Heparin, to keep my blood from clotting and destroying the placenta. While I was relieved not to be starting the long-term steroids, the thought of daily shots for the next eight months was tough to process. I have a terrible needle phobia, and that was a type of semi-torture for me.

David and I made the decision not to reveal the fact that we were pregnant again until we were out of the first trimester. I knew my family and close friends would be

A View from the Parents' Corner

very concerned about me, and quite frankly, their worry would not help them or me. It was very hard keeping such big news from the people I love, but I do believe it was the right decision. The most difficult aspect of this secret was not being able to share my own worries and fears. I suffered with severe morning sickness until eighteen weeks. The sickness became so bad that my doctors finally put me on a drug called Zofran, which is an anti-nausea medication that is given to chemotherapy patients. It was very difficult to take care of the children. They couldn't understand why Mommy had her head in a toilet several times a day, or why she was so tired that she frequently fell asleep while sitting up on the couch. "What's wrong with Mommy? Why does she feel bad so much?" These were questions we had to dodge until we were past thirteen weeks.

One thing that helped me deal psychologically with the ordeal of being extremely sick for months on end was picturing in my mind the baby I was carrying. In my mind, when I saw us together, we were both always healthy and happy. My medical condition makes it necessary to have monthly ultrasounds, so I was able to watch this baby growing with every appointment. In my mind, when I pictured myself holding the baby, I was always holding a baby girl. Something in me just seemed to know that I was carrying a girl. I already knew her name: Lanie. Lanie was a name I had heard in college, and I had always thought that it was a sweet name. Laurie and Lanie just seemed to go together like peanut butter and jelly. I just loved the way it sounded. I tried to keep a distance emotionally from this pregnancy because of the complications we had with Zach, and the risk involved in the pregnancy for both the baby and me. But I couldn't help but love the baby. I was very attached to the idea of the baby and could not even concede the possibility that we might not have a good outcome. Someone asked me how I dealt with the uncertainty of going through a pregnancy with so much risk attached to it. My answer was that I really didn't deal with it at all. If I had really let myself believe that either of us might have a bad outcome, I would never have had a moment of peace, nor would I have been able to do the things that I had to do to take care of my family.

At thirteen weeks, we finally told our children and the rest of the world about our new addition. All of the kids were excited about the new baby, but Laurie was particularly excited. "Will I have a little sister?" she would ask. "We don't know yet. Maybe. But whether it is a new sister or another new brother, we will love the baby with all of our hearts." She hoped with all of her heart that it was a girl, and for her sake, I was hoping that it was, too. The reaction to my pregnancy from my family and friends was a mixed bag. There was a lot of concern for my health, which at times seemed to overshadow the joy of the wonderful event. Even though I understood that the worry and concern were coming from a place of love, it was hard to accept the lack of enthusiasm from those we care about most.

The early part of the pregnancy went by without any serious complications. But in the early part of the second trimester, I began suffering from blinding headaches. Initially my doctors prescribed a medicine that treats migraines. Unfortunately, the drug made me so dizzy I couldn't drive. As an alternative, my doctors advised me to drink a cup of coffee in the morning and a cup in the afternoon. Apparently, the caffeine helps constrict blood flow in the brain, which in turn, helps ease the headaches. I had never had a cup of coffee in my life until my fifth pregnancy. I didn't exactly relish the thought of having to drink coffee. However, it was better than suffering from headaches, so I drank it.

It took a little while to get use to the taste of coffee. But once I did, buddy, I was hooked... stinkin' rotten hooked. (I hang my head in shame as I type this... addiction in any form is just plain ugly!) I can remember a time, not so long ago, when I used to make fun of all the little stupid sheep following the flock into Starbuck's to pay four dollars for a cup of coffee. In my opinion, a four dollar cup of coffee was the greatest marketing dupe pulled on the public since people paid money for pet rocks back in the 1970's. One cup of coffee per day could cost you more money in a month than a car payment... it's crazy.

Well, it wasn't long before I learned to go "Bah, Bah...." and joined the rest of the flock in line. If I could've started an I.V. line and hung a bag of it, I probably would have. The coffee controlled my headaches and the caffeine "pick me up" allowed me to slap an "S" on my chest and leap over tall buildings in a single bound. Okay, maybe that's an exaggeration, but it did help me fight the profound fatigue, and enabled me to do the things I needed to do for my family during the day.

At my fourteen week ultrasound, I pestered the technician, Sherry, to see if she could tell the sex of the baby. I was ready to call this baby either Lanie or Will. She hesitated and said that she didn't like to call the sex before sixteen weeks. I am persistent, however, and she agreed to try to see. The baby was wiggling, turning and swimming all over the place. Dr. Raimer came over to get a look and she couldn't get a good peek either. "I just can't say for sure.." she kept repeating. "Well, what do you THINK it is?" But she wouldn't call it. "Okay" I said. "You just aim it between the legs, and I'll make the call. I'll know a penis if I see one!" I declared. But this little baby was not going to cooperate and finally we had to stop trying to look. I was completely disappointed, and began to wipe the gel off of my stomach and pulled myself together to leave. Sherry could see how disappointed I was.

As I was getting up to leave she said, "Hey Laura, if I had to make a guess, I'd say it's probably a girl." "How sure are you?" "Eighty percent" she said. I left that office grinning from ear to ear. I thought those were pretty good odds and from that moment on, David and I started calling her Lanie between ourselves. At eighteen weeks, her sex was confirmed and we told Laurie the news she had been dreaming about... she was finally going to have a sister!

At twenty weeks it became necessary for me to begin wearing a maternity belt. Five pregnancies in nine years had left the ligaments in my abdomen very weak, and made it difficult to support the weight of the advancing pregnancy. By the beginning of the third trimester, it had become very difficult to move without pain. As the last weeks of the pregnancy crept by, the effects of aging (being mid-thirties) in combination with multiple pregnancies, was taking its toll. The effects of the shots were also becoming an issue. The tissue in my arms, legs, and stomach had been damaged from the daily injections, and I began to have problems with excessive bleeding at the injection sites.

At thirty six weeks, the decision was made to stop my Heparin in preparation for the upcoming delivery. Without stopping the Heparin, the possibility of hemorrhaging and other complications increases dramatically. At my thirty-seven week appointment, I went in to have an amniocentesis to check lung maturity, in preparation to induce labor. But when I went in for the appointment, I was so needle phobic from all of the injections I had received, I just couldn't go through with it. An ultrasound showed that Lanie's placenta was still healthy, as was the cord flow between her and me, and her fluid levels were normal. Dr. Raimer said if we waited a week to induce, we wouldn't need the amnio, so we waited and checked into the hospital at thirty eight weeks.

On the morning of February 19, Dr. Raimer came by my room around 9:00 am to check me. I was so glad that she was on call that morning. Even though I liked all of the doctors in the practice, she was always my favorite. She has seven biological children of her own, and she is my hero. Anytime someone made me feel like I was crazy or a stupid southern girl for having so many kids, I'd just think of Dr. Raimer and say "Well, Dr. Raimer has seven, and I know she is smart, and definitely not crazy!"

When Dr. Raimer checked me that morning, my cervix was dilated to three centimeters and I was already having steady contractions. "I will go ahead and break your water, and we will get the epidural on board." she said. After breaking my water, she said she would see me later in the day. "I told her I'd be seeing her in about two hours. She just smiled and left. Moments later, the anesthesiologist came by and gave me the epidural of my dreams. Bless Dr. Martyr... if I ever have another baby, I will schedule my induction around HIS schedule.

Exactly an hour after Dr. Raimer broke my water, I was completely dilated. My nurse ran down the hall to page Dr. Raimer and I waited with David for both of them to return. Up to that point, I had been feeling pretty good. But as the baby was rapidly descending into the birth canal, and my contractions intensified, a serious wave of nausea hit me. I told David "I'm going to be stomach sick." "Which way?" he asked. "Both" I answered. Just then, Dr. Raimer and my nurse came in and hurriedly prepped me for a fast delivery. "I am going to be sick." I said. The nurse stuck a bucket next to my head and I felt green. This had to go down as one of my life's most embarrassing moments. I'm laying here with my legs in stirrups, in the presence of my husband, the nurse, and my favorite doctor, and my body was betraying me in embarrassing ways. Labor and delivery is no easy gig, physically or emotionally. Everyone in the room assured me (except David) that they see this all the time, but you know what... it doesn't make it any less uncomfortable to hear that!

Finally the urge to be ill passed, and I got down to pushing. Between the size of the baby, my weak pelvic muscles and a really good epidural, I was struggling to push Lanie out. After forty five minutes of pushing, Dr. Raimer finally put some "goop" (her words, not mine) around the perimeter of Lanie's head to grease it up, hoping to help her slide out. I bore down with all my might, and hollered at Dr. Raimer to grab Lanie by her ears the next time her head came forward... I didn't want her sliding back inside! Finally, one last push at exactly 11:25 am and our beautiful Lanie was born. Dr. Raimer pulled her out and placed her on my stomach. I reached down to pull her close to my face and she promptly peed on me! I couldn't believe how big she looked. At seven pounds, twelve ounces, she was our biggest baby. I was also tickled that she looked so much like me. I kept whispering to her "Just look at you! Just look at how perfect you are! I'm your mommy and I love you!" I guess there is just some part of me, deep down inside, that can't fully believe everything is going to be fine until I hold that baby in my arms, until I feel that little breath on my face.

"Congratulations, Laura" Dr. Raimer said. "She's beautiful. What's her full name?" David and I chuckled for a moment. "We are planning to name her Melanie Suzanne and calling her Lanie, but the middle name might be in jeopardy." Our plan was for her middle name to be Suzanne, after my sister. But my sister and I had been squabbling in the days before the birth, and we were not too happy with each other at that point. "I hope we don't have to come up with an alternative" I said. However, a sweet congratulatory call from Suzanne within an hour of Lanie's birth smoothed everything over, and Miss Lanie was legally Melanie Suzanne Hull.

Dr. Raimer finished collecting the cord blood, as we had done with our other children, and soon I was sent to my room, while Lanie went to the nursery for her newborn workup. We had brought party supplies to the hospital with us to have a birthday party for Lanie that night with our family. David decorated the room with pink crepe paper and balloons, and we had ordered a birthday cake from a local bakery. Six o'clock that night, David brought our children, along with my mother, to the hospital to meet Lanie and to have a birthday party for her. Hearing four little precious voices sing "Happy birthday, dear Lanie..." on the very day of her birth, is a special memory for me. Within the next hour, however, I was exhausted, and bleeding heavily, so the party was cut short. But the children had a wonderful time welcoming Miss Lanie into our family, and I was relieved to have her here safe and sound.

The day Lanie and I were scheduled to leave the hospital, Dr. Montenegro from my OB group came by to give me a final check before I left. At that point he informed me that the decision had been made to have me resume Heparin shots for the next six weeks. I was extremely disappointed, but the fact that my blood clots too easily made me a candidate for a pulmonary embolism until six weeks postpartum. I reluctantly agreed to restart the shots, but it only fueled a problem I could already feel beginning: postpartum depression.

Let me sing you a chorus of "I'm not crazy, I'm just a little unwell..." Postpartum depression came on with a vengeance. I never really had a significant problem with postpartum depression with the other children, but I had battled the blues to some degree throughout this pregnancy, probably due largely to the profound fatigue and extreme sickness. Within five days of delivery, I knew I was having a problem. As the sun started to go down just before six o'clock each evening, I would start to feel a "dark cloud" park over my head, almost like clockwork. I tried to stay busy during those pre-dinner hours, but anxiety crept up inside me and made it hard to do anything. As much as I was enjoying Lanie, I was feeling overwhelmed by the physical exhaustion of nursing an infant all night, and from taking care of five children all

A View from the Parents' Corner

day. My mother had stayed with me for the first ten days after Lanie and I came home from the hospital, but my sister, Suzanne, delivered her first child right after Lanie was born, so she had to leave to help Suzanne. David took the next week off, but after that, I was on my own. I have wonderful friends who offered to come over and help me out during the day, but I was really having problems with the blues, and just didn't want my friends to see how much I was struggling with it, so I kept to myself.

It finally got to the point that when David came home from work, around six o'clock, I instructed him to feed the kids and take care of the night routine, while I locked myself in our bedroom, buried my face in a pillow and cried until 8:00. At that point, the "dark cloud" would dissipate and I'd feel like myself again. My doctors encouraged me to start an anti-depressant to help handle the stress I was enduring. They were concerned that my post-delivery fatigue, in combination with my lupus, could cause me to crash, both physically and emotionally. Ultimately, I refused the medication due to the fact that I was breastfeeding and couldn't settle in with exposing Lanie to an anti-depressant through my milk. Knowing the depression would most likely be temporary, I decided to just try to live through it. I knew that David, my parents, my sisters, and close friends were worried. I was struggling and they could see it, but had little power to help. As our twelve year wedding anniversary was approaching in March, my sweet David made a touching gesture and bought me a gift that I had always wanted: a seven person Jacuzzi. It was a "thank you for twelve years of marriage/thank you for our five beautiful children/please get over your postpartum depression, you are scaring me" present. I was very much looking forward to breaking in that Jacuzzi with my husband on a cool, starry night, but that would have to wait a few months. Fortunately, by six weeks post delivery, the depression subsided and I was glad that I hadn't started the depression medication.

Lanie made her own place in our home very quickly. She was the first child to make it to "the big bed", between Mommy and Daddy. As much as I preached against the "freshman mistake" of putting a baby in the big bed, my desperation for sleep provoked me to do it. Lanie was the first child I had who wanted to be held constantly. I found myself doing all of my housework with her in a snuggly... vacuuming, folding clothes, dusting. The only housework I would not do with her against me was cooking. The cord between us had been cut, but she didn't seem to realize it. My song for Miss Lanie is "Hey, hey Lanie! I want to know... if you'll be my girl!" to the tune of "Hey Baby". She loves me to sing this song to her. I carry her around (all day) singing this song!

Lanie is also my first certified pacifier baby. Chad enjoyed a pacifier only during his newborn days, then switched over to the thumb. Our other children were all thumb suckers as well, and we have already incurred orthodontic bills as a result. But Lanie took to the pacifier immediately, and seemingly, permanently. What a wonderful invention that is... a mouth plug! (sometimes I wish they had adult versions of those!) All I can say is that it is a good thing the companies who make pacifiers don't charge as much as they are worth... because we would gladly pay any amount of money for the peace and quiet that a pacifier brings to our home.

A View from the Parents' Corner

The birth of Lanie only re-affirmed what we already knew... that we love having a large family, and that there is enough room and enough love for each new wonderful addition. I can't imagine ever getting to a point of holding our baby (or any of my children, for that matter) and thinking "Whew! I never want to go through that again." Some people just have a sense of when they are "done" and that the family is complete. I'm not sure we will get to that point voluntarily. I am in my mid-thirties, so age and other health related issues have come into play. I know that there's not an abundance of years left to have more children, so we may or may not have child number six. Whether or not we do will have nothing to do with a lack of desire to have more. Still, I'm not in a hurry to fly through these baby days. As crazy and hectic as they are at times, they are also profoundly wonderful. The fatigue fades (eventually), but the wonderful memories will not.

Our Lanie

Crayon Marks on a Gutsy Heart

25. The Lion, The Monkey, Two Princesses, And A Doodle-Doo

I am always amazed at the fact that children raised in the same house, at the same time, in basically the same way, can turn out so differently. This was true in my family when I was growing up. My sister Suzanne and I are almost exactly three years apart in age and we couldn't be more different if we had been raised on different ends of the earth. My blond hair/blue eyes to her black hair/brown eyes is only where the differences begin. Why is that so often the case in many households? It's that nature vs. nurture argument, and I tend to agree more with the nature argument most of the time.

In raising five children, it's been interesting to study the various genetic combinations David and I have created. Please don't take that statement the wrong way. It sounds far more clinical or scientific than I intend. But it is admittedly interesting to ponder the fact that these children who are so closely alike genetically, very close in age, and being raised as a group together in a large household, could be so different in temperament, personalities, their outlook on life and the way they process their world around them.

Our son Chad made an interesting observation when he was merely pre-school age. I asked him one time "If you were an animal, what kind of animal would you be?" He sat for a moment and thought about my question, but then answered matter-of-factly that he was a lion and then went on to add that his brother Joey was a monkey. I had to chuckle, for if I had answered that question myself, those are exactly the same animals I would have used to describe our boys.

Chad is my lion. He's the quiet, but deliberate leader of the pack. He's very even tempered and not prone to wild swings in mood or behavior. Even as an infant this was his disposition. When he was born, he was very calm and observant of his surroundings. It took a lot of stimulation to upset him as a baby, and this is still true today. As a young child, Chad was easy, easy, easy to deal with. He was fully potty trained by his second birthday because he was so easy to teach. Today, he tends to be a quiet observer. He internalizes the things around him and tends to be a very gentle, sensitive soul. When Chad was young, David traveled five days out of every week. During the times David was gone, Chad literally grieved for David. Even at the age of two, he was sensitive enough to experience a deep sense of loss when his daddy was absent. Still today, Chad absorbs his environment more than our other children. Things don't always roll off of Chad as quickly as the other children. His attitudes seem particularly influenced by television and movies and we are careful to police this in our home. When Chad was in pre-k, his teacher asked him what he wanted to be when he grew up. Without hesitating he quoted a line from Star Wars "I want to be a Jedi knight, like my father before me."

I can see various traits in Chad that I know he inherited from different family members. It's not always easy to read Chad; it's not always easy to guess what he is thinking. That is a trait he gets straight from me. But for the most part, Chad is very much like David. His thought processes and interests are very similar, as is the way he learns. Chad isn't one to get overly excited when something good happens, but he shows disappointment all over his face when something "bad" happens. The first time we moved away from family was when Chad was two and a half, almost three. He has always been very close to my parents and both of my sisters. When we moved away from Atlanta in 1997, Chad didn't understand why his grandparents and aunts were no longer around everyday. He felt a sense of abandonment from them. One night when I tucked him into bed, about one week after our move, I listened to Chad say his prayers. I noticed that he had left the entire side of my family out of his prayer. "Don't you want to pray for Mimi, Big Daddy, Susie, and Katie?" I asked him. "No!" he said. "They are not around anymore, so they are off my prayer list!" Poor little guy couldn't comprehend that HE was actually the one who moved away, not my parents and sisters. All he knew was that he was mad at them for not being around anymore. The reason why was irrelevant to him. Eventually, they made it back on to the prayer list, but it took a few weeks.

Chad has a realistic, no-nonsense approach to life which, at times, is funny to watch. One Christmas a few years ago, my mother was on an ornament buying craze. She bought literally dozens of keepsake ornaments as gifts that year, and gave them not only to David and me, but the kids as well. Each of the kids took turns opening their gifts from their grandparents on Christmas morning, but by the time Chad had opened gift number three or four that did not bear an action figure or some other cool toy, but rather a pile of ornaments, he was frustrated. As Joey reached to open a package that was obviously not a toy, Chad grabbed his hand and warned Joey, as if imminent danger was looming, "Dooon't touch it, Joey... it's another ornament!"

Chad cuts to the chase, does not beat around the bush, and does not shovel a lot of manure, if you know what I mean. (It would actually serve him well to learn to "politic" a little more). He is the kind of kid who loves "the tough guys". John Wayne would have been his hero. Cowboys on horses and shootouts in the middle of town would be his idea of entertainment. He would never like some sissy singing, guitar playing, cowboy. I remember my father complaining about "wussy" cowboys like Gene Autry, who would go and mess up a perfectly good gun fight by breaking into song. Our Chad can relate to that kind of mentality. He is enough like his grandfather that way.

I think dancing is a wonderful skill for any child to have, but especially for a boy. I feel it does a lot for a kid's self esteem and makes him much less self-conscious in social situations. I enrolled Chad and his brother in a hip hop dancing class, and immediately met resistance from Chad. After the first lesson he declared the experience to be "the worst thing that has ever happened to me!" (If that is truly the worst thing that has ever happened to him, he is doing well...by the way, I withdrew him from the class that very night). John Wayne would not have hip hopped, a Jedi Knight would never hip hop dance, a lion would never hip hop dance and neither would Chad Hull. (apparently)

My lion is protective of our pride. He is very gentle and sweet with the babies, and very capable of taking care of their basic needs. There is a very tender side to Chad that is dear to watch when he is interacting with his younger siblings. One time when Laurie was still an infant, I overheard Chad whispering to her, "Don't worry, Laurie... I will always protect you from the bad guys." I have seen him defend both Joey and Laurie when he felt that other children were being unkind or unfair. I feel that he is an ideal role model for my younger children to look up to and I know that when push comes to shove, Chad will always step up to the plate. My tough little lion has a very tender heart, and I am proud that he is the leader of the pack.

When my Joey was born, I knew he was different from Chad as far as temperament goes, right out of the box. He had been a very reactive baby while I was pregnant, and I remember not sleeping much the entire third trimester because he rolled around so much. His entrance into this world was markedly different than Chad's. He came out bellowing, mad as a wet hen about being taken out of his mommy's nice warm body. In his first act of defiance, he peed about a gallon on the doctor who delivered him, then proceeded to wail until he was wrapped up in a blanket and placed in my arms. He was a beautiful, sweet baby, but not a calm baby. He cried... a lot! I remember holding Joey in my arms around the two week mark, and looking down at his beautiful little face and thinking "you need to learn to control your temper, or we are going to have a hard time getting along." Of course, I was sleep deprived and weary, but his colic was hard to handle.

Eventually he outgrew the colic, but he was still a demanding baby. When it came time to begin potty training, he had no interest in it whatsoever. He was over the age of three before he was toilet trained. But even once he was trained, he wouldn't stop to go to the bathroom. He was definitely anal retentive (don't know where he got that from!) and after three days of retention, he would deposit a foot-long snake in the potty. Joey is a very gifted child, and experts say that those children tend to be harder to handle. It was not that Joey was unusually difficult, it's just that Chad was unusually easy, and that spoiled us. By the time Joey was pre-school age, most of the "difficulties" had resolved themselves and what remained was a wonderful child, with a very different temperament, personality, and approach to life than his brother.

It would be fair to say that Joey is "our little monkey". From a very early age, Joey was the rambunctious one... and I mean that very affectionately. He loved to run, climb, laugh loud, be silly and always had some kind of nonsense going on. He's definitely my "extreme child." When Joey is happy, he's the easiest, most happy go-lucky kid on earth; but when he's unhappy, his world falls apart... he gets mad, mad, MAD! Joey's the kind of kid who will "swing first and ask questions later" if he feels he's been wronged. But on the flip side, Joey has an unusually sweet spirit. Man! He is a politician in the making!

Joey figured out early in life that he could capitalize on the mistakes of his siblings. He is quick to point out that "he is my good boy, while the others are..." (you get the point). If one child is getting in trouble for whining, he will make sure that I realize that "I didn't whine, I did what you asked me to". Or if one of the other kids has complained about the dinner on the table, Joey is quick to say "I'll eat it, Mommy. I like everything you cook!" It's funny to watch Joey when he is in this mode. I know I'm being completely schmoozed, but I enjoy it anyway. Joey learned a very valuable social skill early in life... buttering people up can get you far. He has used this to his advantage many times, and he is quite the charmer. But he's never consciously manipulative, and that's what makes it so funny.

Joey has an innate sense of fair play, that probably exceeds that of our other children. When Joey was in Kindergarten, the assistant teacher met me at the car one day and said, "Laura, I just have to tell you how sweet your Joey is." She then recounted a story of how someone had brought a bag of candy into the classroom to share with the classmates. Apparently, there was enough candy for the students, but not for the teachers. Joey became very concerned that his teachers didn't have candy, and offered his candy to them. He didn't think it was fair that his teachers had not received the treats as well, and was worried that their feelings would be hurt. This didn't surprise me at all. Joey never wants anyone to feel hurt or left out. He's very thoughtful and loving and has a unique sincerity in his manner. He has a wide eyed wonder about everything.

It's a joy to watch Joey discover something new or to receive something he has been wanting. He's so appreciative of everything given to him. It makes me feel especially good to do nice things for Joey because it means so much to him. His excitement about life is contagious. His happiness and self confidence show in everything he does. He has a wonderful imagination and thinks that everything "is amazing". I hope he will always keep that wide-eyed wonder about life, and I hope he will always have that wonderful self-confidence that just screams "I'm a winner" to everyone he meets. Joey wears his heart, and his emotions on his sleeve, which I think serves his personality well. He may not be a lion in terms of his temperament, but he has a lion-sized heart.

My Laurie girl is definitely a princess. Laurie is a girly-girl. I was a major tomboy growing up, and I had no idea that I could give birth to such a dainty little lady. Laurie was a very calm, even tempered baby, much like Chad. By the time she hit the toddler years, I could definitely see the difference between our girl and the boys. Anyone who says there is not a difference in the way little girls and little boys play at this age must be smoking something. Don't let anyone fool you into thinking that society "conditions" little boys and girls to play a certain way. Our boys came out of the box ready to play rough and tumble, just as our daughter came out ready to nurture her baby dolls. At the age of two years, three months, I was very pregnant with Zach, when my sister Suzanne came down to Florida to visit us. On that trip, Suzanne and Laurie bonded over make up and nail polish. I have the cutest picture of my little Laurie applying eye-make up on my sister (and doing a surprisingly good job, I might add).

Laurie likes all of the stereotypical girl things. She loves to play dress up and have tea parties. She loves to play with Barbie dolls and princesses. She likes to take care of her baby dolls and play house. She has a collection of "beautiful things", which is a box full of make-up, costume jewelry, and other little trinkets she considers beautiful. Her favorite color is pink and she loves taking ballet and tap dancing. But this year, five year old Laurie added cheerleading to the list of things she loves to do. Yes, my little Laurie takes cheerleading and she's very good at it. The first time I watched her perform a routine with her group, it hit me "Oh my, I've given birth to a cheerleader!" As a former athlete, who never really considered cheerleading a "sport," I was floored that I could have given birth to a little pompom queen. But she is the cutest little pompom queen I've ever seen, and I get a real kick out of watching her perform.

My little Laurie is sandwiched between three brothers, but she holds her own with them quite nicely. In fact, this little princess rules the play kingdom much of the time. It's fun to watch her play with her older brothers. She's more than willing to play GI Joe or air hockey with them, but they will not return the favor by playing dress up or Barbie with her. Poor little Laurie. She wanted a sister to play dress up. I was so happy for her when we found out that we were going to have another little girl. Now she is just waiting for Lanie to get big enough to play with her.

Laurie has a very gentle, quiet, thoughtful nature. She has a very sweet, easy-going personality, and a quiet confidence that is disarming. She is very easy to get along with, but certainly not a pushover. Her advanced vocabulary and imagination leads me to believe that I don't know half of what that little girl has stored up in her head. David and I joke that she is going to be our little tap-dancing neurosurgeon when she grows up. Laurie is like a little sponge and picks up things so easily. In many ways, Laurie is a stereotypical middle child. Because she is so quiet by nature, it's sometimes easy for her to get lost in the shuffle when everyone's needs are needing to be met at once. Of all the children, she seems to be the one who craves time alone with me the most. She always wants me to play dress up with her, or to read to her or play a board game. Unfortunately, I'm not able to give her as much one-on-one time as she would like, and I have to make a deliberate effort to pay attention to her subtle cues that say, "Mommy, I need you now." I think my Laurie is both beautiful and brilliant, and I fully expect to be cheering on the front row of her graduation from medical school one day.

My Zach is quite a little character. Very early on, David nicknamed him "Zach-a-doodle-doo". Even today, we still call him "Doodle-doo", which seems to fit his personality perfectly. Zach is our blender child. It is as if you put Chad and Joey into a blender and out popped Zach. I see traits of both boys in Zach. He is a typical two year old... funny, inquisitive, prone to an occasional temper tantrum, and completely opposed to the idea of wearing "big boy pants". Given his strong will and bad temper, I can see him graduating from college wearing the world's biggest diaper.

Zach's chief playmate is Laurie, so he gets dressed up like a princess far more than David is comfortable with. I told my husband to relax... Zach is all boy; but it is funny to see him come into a room all dolled up like his sister. I believe some of my husband's discomfort with Zach's feminine play was put to rest lately when he spotted Zach sitting in the floor, playing with a toy dinosaur and a Barbie doll. Zach's end of the conversation went something like this: ROAR! EAT BARBIE! and in a testosterone charged moment, he proceeded to have the T-Rex chomp down on Barbie's head.

It's a pleasure to watch Zach play. He takes such delight in everything. He has a contagious smile and laugh. There is nothing I enjoy doing more than watching him swing at the park or chase birds at the beach. He is a boy with a heart full of joy, and he has a wonderful sense of humor. I see so much of both Chad and Joey in him. It is almost like reliving parts of their early childhood through him. I had almost forgotten how nice it is to have a "little" boy again. It is wonderful to watch him grow and learn, and discover his world around him. And my favorite three words in the world "Love you, Mommy" are ones he says to me frequently. It melts my heart every time. He isn't really to the age where I can write a lot about the "type" of child he is, as a lot has yet to be revealed. But every day is a joy with our Zach-a-doodle-doo... my little boy with a heart full of joy, and a smile that can light up the world.

Miss Lanie is the latest princess born into our family. All of our children have little nicknames and Lanie is called "Miss Belle" (as in "The belle of the ball"). When I was a child, my grandfather always called me "Laura Belle". It was his sweet little name for me... his little southern belle. It just seemed appropriate to nickname our precious and beautiful second little princess "Lanie Belle". Lanie is a delight. A huge point in her favor... she looks like me. Okay, I know that is really vain, but after five really rough pregnancies, and four other children who have my husband's beautiful face stamped all over them, I wanted at least one child that people would see and say "Wow! She really looks like her mother, doesn't she?" Well, Miss Lanie really does look like her Mommy, and I'm not ashamed to admit that I LOVE IT! My mother says that Lanie's temperament is much like mine was as a baby. She is playful, and at times a little aggressive. She has a good sense of humor and can tell when you are trying to be playful with her. She smiles incessantly and lights up like a Christmas tree when one of her siblings sits in the floor to play with her. She's inquisitive and determined and "in to everything". She can be a little pistol when she wants to be, but she is sweet as pie, and certainly the apple of my eye.

So far, Miss Belle has hit all of her developmental milestones early. She began crawling at four months of age and began pulling up at seven months, walking with help at eight months. She is very alert and doesn't have a great need for excessive amounts of sleep. She didn't start sleeping through the night consistently until the age of eight months, but she has adjusted well to the demanding routine of our household. My mother says she is quite a bit like me, and I choose to look at that as a positive thing. If that is so, then she will keep me on my toes, that's for sure. But I know that I will enjoy the experience that goes along with it.

All five of our children are very different, unique individuals. Their individuality is not lost due to the fact that they spend the majority of their time as a group. We are very blessed that their differences actually complement each other very well most of the time. Even though our household is frequently loud, and trying at times, each of these little lives is a joy to watch unfold. No one can "parent" their children into being just alike, and no one should ever try. The fact that a group of children, raised at the same time, in basically the same way, could still hold on to their individuality is a great unexplainable miracle of life, and certainly, at least in our home, scores a point for "nature" in the nature vs. nurture argument. We feel that we parent our children equally (or at least close to the same), but they are five very different people, and that is a wonder to behold.

A View from the Parents' Corner   237

"Parenthood is a truly wonderful exhaustion, experienced in the reality of days spent living life fully, with meaning, a definite purpose, and extreme joy."

Conclusion

When the parent/child relationship is healthy, the view from the Parents' Corner should be a beautiful one. The journey along the winding road of parenthood is not always easy, just as the journey through childhood is not always easy. The journey through parenthood never really ends, but changes once the children are grown. I remember my mother telling me when I was pregnant with my first child that once he was born, I'd never draw another free breath in this life, and that I'd never want to. Oh how true these words are. I know that my children will grow up and have lives of their own someday, but as long as I live, they will always be a factor in any major decisions I make in my life. I will never again have the freedoms I possessed before I became a mother and I wouldn't want that freedom back if I could have it. The protective instincts I have as a mother will never go away, though I'm sure I'll have to learn to suppress them to a small degree once the children are grown. I will always "go to bat" for my children, and will always "cover their backs" when they need me. Everyone needs someone in this life that he/she knows in the bottom of his heart will always be there for him. I consider this my charge in life. I can't foresee this ever changing. My children will have my help, my support, and my love for as long as I draw a breath in this life. That's my promise to them.

When our children lay their heads down on their pillows at night, there are things I hope they go to sleep knowing in the depths of their hearts:

1. I want them to know down to the core of their being

that I love them unconditionally. The love a parent feels for a child is the only truly unconditional love that exists. I want them to know that I will be a source of strength for them; that I am strong enough to help them carry any weight they must bear in life. I am capable of handling anything negative that might happen; they will never need to protect me or my feelings. I am the one who is here to help and protect them. I want them to know that there is nothing they could ever say or do that would change the way I feel about them or the way that I see them. They can feel secure in the fact that I will never withhold my love from them. I may not always agree with the decisions they make in their lives, but they will never lose my love as a result of them.

2. I want them to know that they should feel life fully. The world can be such a wonderful place. Great amounts of joy and happiness exist all around us. I hope I have taught our children to experience that happiness and joy to the fullest. On the flip side, there is also sorrow in this life. I hope I have provided a place of security and comfort for my children, so they know that it's okay to express their sorrow as well. I hope they know that they don't always have to "toughen up"; it is most certainly okay to cry. Feelings aren't something to fear, and the expression of those feelings, as long as it is done in a healthy way, is something I hope they will always feel comfortable doing.

3. I want my children to know how happy and proud they make me every day of their lives. I have said this at various points in this book, but this point bears repeating over and over again. I want my children to know, that they know, that they know... that I consider it an honor and privilege to be charged with the upbringing of such

wonderful human beings. There is nothing else I could have ever done with my life that would have brought me the kind of happiness and fulfillment I experience in being their mother. The pride I feel in watching these young lives unfold, as new chapters in life begin for them, is almost indescribable. I tell them every night when I tuck them into bed how much I love them, how proud I am of them, and how happy they make me. I hope they internalize that; at least in a subconscious way.

Parenting young children is full of wild and crazy moments. I recently sent my sister, Suzanne, who is a first time mom, a card advising her to cherish every wild and crazy moment, as they go by way too fast. The years spent raising our children, in my opinion, are truly the golden years. I am in no hurry for this time in my life to pass by, though it is going by very quickly. I treasure in my heart every new experience with my children, and the photographs in my mind of our lives together during these wonderful days won't ever fade with time.

If I could have you take away one concept from reading this book it would be this: Parenthood is a truly wonderful exhaustion, experienced in the reality of days spent living life fully... with meaning... a definite purpose... and extreme joy. Real parenting is rarely easy, but it's frequently wonderful and always fulfilling. When the focus is in the home where it should be, the view from the Parents' Corner is always beautiful.

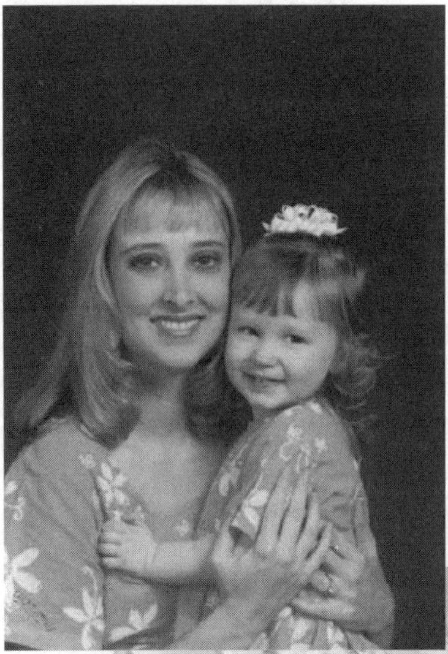

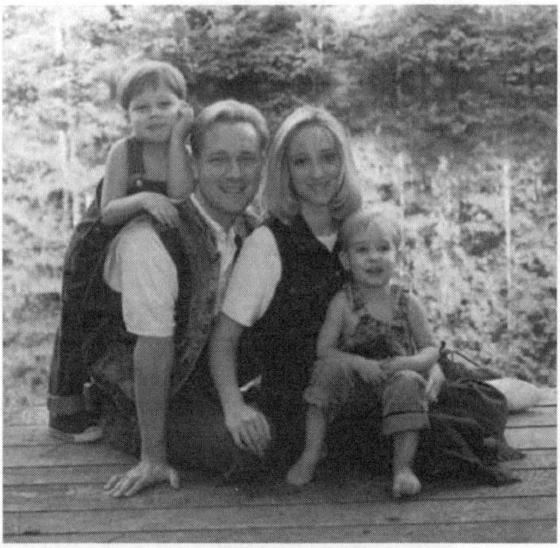

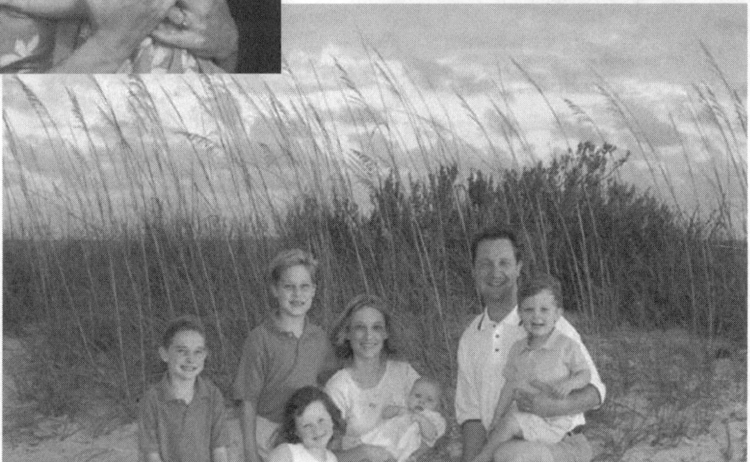

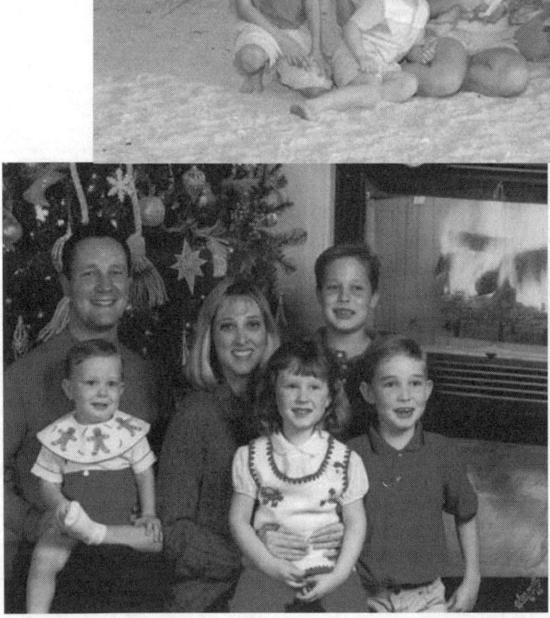

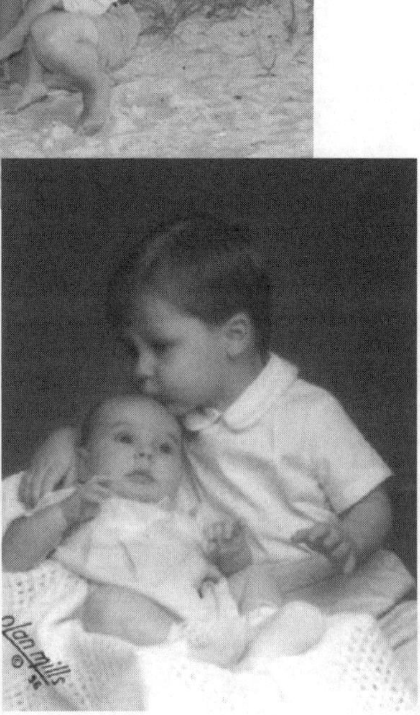
olan mills